New Directions in Metal Clay

New Directions in Metal Clay

Intermediate Techniques: Stone Setting, Enameling, Surface Design & More

CeCe Wire

LARK BOOKS

A Division of Sterling Publishing Co., Inc.
New York / London

Editor: James Knight
Art Director: Kathleen Holmes
Cover Designer: Cindy LaBreacht
Assistant Editor: Susan Keiffer
Associate Art Director: Shannon Yokeley
Art Production Assistants: Jeff Hamilton,
  Travis Medford
Editorial Assistance: Delores Gosnell
Illustrator: Olivier Rollin
Photographers: Steve Mann, Stewart O'Shields

Dedication

I proudly dedicate this book
to my very cool parents,
Daniel and Deborah Wire,
known to their friends as
"Crude and Prude."

The Library of Congress has cataloged the hardcover edition as follows:
Wire, CeCe.
   New directions in metal clay : 25 creative jewelry projects / CeCe Wire.
     p. cm.
   Includes index.
   ISBN-13: 978-1-57990-489-0 (hc-plc with jacket : alk. paper)
   ISBN-10: 1-57990-489-0 (hc-plc with jacket : alk. paper)
   1. Jewelry making. 2. Precious metal clay. I. Title.
 TT212.W58   2007
 739.27—dc22

                                        2006100863

10 9 8 7 6 5 4 3 2 1

Published by Lark Books, A Division of Sterling Publishing Co., Inc.
387 Park Avenue South, New York, N.Y. 10016

First Paperback Edition 2009
Text © 2007, CeCe Wire
Photography © 2007, Lark Books, A Division of Sterling Publishing Co., Inc.
Illustrations © 2007, Lark Books, A Division of Sterling Publishing Co., Inc.

Previously published as New Directions in Metal Clay: 25 Creative Jewelry Projects

Distributed in Canada by Sterling Publishing, c/o Canadian Manda Group,
165 Dufferin Street Toronto, Ontario, Canada M6K 3H6

Distributed in the United Kingdom by GMC Distribution Services, Castle Place,
166 High Street, Lewes, East Sussex, England BN7 1XU

Distributed in Australia by Capricorn Link (Australia) Pty Ltd.,
P.O. Box 704, Windsor, NSW 2756 Australia

If you have questions or comments about this book, please contact:
Lark Books
67 Broadway
Asheville, NC 28801
(828) 253-0467

Manufactured in China

ISBN 13: 978-1-57990-489-0 (hardcover) 978-1-60059-546-2 (paperback)

For information about custom editions, special sales, premium and corporate purchases, please contact Sterling Special Sales Department at 800-805-5489 or specialsales@sterlingpub.com.

Contents

Introduction
Discovering the Magic of Metal Clay

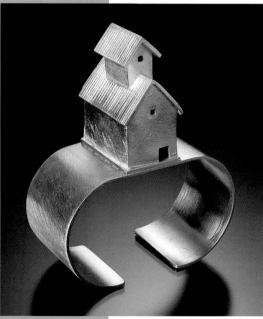

I was first introduced to metal clay in 1995 when I read a magazine article written by artist, author, publisher, and renaissance man Tim McCreight. The information in the article kept me up all night, and I filled a sketchbook with ideas I was anxious to explore.

I was just finishing a graduate program in jewelry and metalsmithing, so it was the perfect time to be introduced to a revolutionary new material. I was young, over-educated, and jobless, but open to the possibilities of a new way of working with precious metals. I had worked in a fabulously equipped jewelry studio, and I was intrigued by the minimal amount of tools and equipment metal clay required.

I started my journey working with metal clay brimming with enthusiasm. I was embarking on a path that would change my life.

I wrote this book to introduce you to the artistic freedom metal clay offers. First, we'll explore the differences between the available formulas of metal clay and discuss techniques that will help you make the most of each variety. Then, we'll look at ways of setting up your workspace and cover the basics of working with this fascinating material. Finally, step-by-step instructions will guide you through the creation of some beautiful metal clay pieces.

Two of the latest formulas of metal clay, what I call Second Generation and Next Generation metal clay, provide more flexibility in firing times than the original formula. These metal clays allow for some innovative new techniques that yield stunning results. Take a look at the fire-in-place stone settings featured on the Garnet and Silver Necklace on page 133, the vibrant epoxy inlays in the Bauhaus Bold Pin on page 82, or, one of my favorites, the glass inclusions on the Domino Theory Earrings on page 76. The newest formula of gold metal clay allows artists to combine silver and gold on the same piece more easily than ever before. You can see an example of this powerful combination in the Golden Ivy Bracelet on page 110.

Please keep in mind: Metal clay is a very forgiving medium. If you get started on a piece and don't like where it's heading artistically, ball it up and start again. Metal clay begs the artist to play and explore. Don't be afraid to try new things as you move through the projects in this book. If you get an idea for another way of accomplishing something, or if you suddenly decide to take a piece in a new direction, go for it. That's what this book is all about.

I continue to meet people who share my enthusiasm for metal clay. I hope working with metal clay will be a life-altering experience for you as well.

Opposite top: CeCe Wire
La Fayette Granary, 2005
5 x 4.3 x 1 cm
Fine and sterling silver
Photo by Robert Diamante

Opposite bottom: CeCe Wire
Barn with Cupola, 2004
8 x 6.3 x 2.8 cm
Fine and sterling silver
Photo by Robert Diamante

This page, clockwise from upper left: CeCe Wire
Horse Barn, 2003
5.3 x 4.3 x 2.3 cm
Fine and sterling silver
Photo by Robert Diamante

CeCe Wire
Solo Silo, 2002
4.5 x 2 x 1 cm
Fine and sterling silver
Photo by Robert Diamante

CeCe Wire
Tower Road Silos, 2002
4 x 6 x 1.5 cm
Fine and sterling silver
Photo by Robert Diamante

CHAPTER 1

Metal Clay Formulas

You may be asking yourself, "Just what is metal clay?" If you want to impress your friends, tell them it's a powdered metal technological revolution—because that's exactly what it is. The three ingredients in most metal clays are pure silver (or gold) powder, organic binder, and water. Water and binder are what hold the pure metal particles together, making a soft malleable substance much like modeling clay. You can roll it out, model it, cut it, join or assemble separate pieces of it, then texture it and fire it. After firing, what's left is gold or silver that can be polished or finished in a variety of ways.

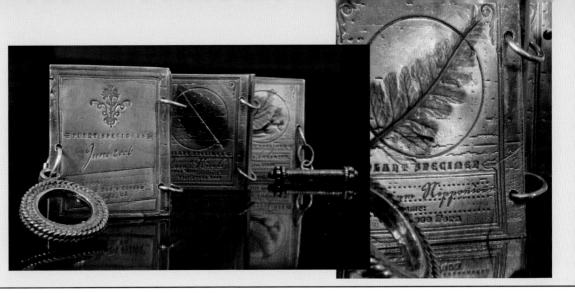

Patrik Kusek
Botanical Specimen Bracelet,
2006
18 x 4 cm
Silver metal clay, photopolymer
plates, leaves; hand-painted
Photo by the artist

Types of Metal Clay

There are now three main versions of metal clay to choose from—the original formula (referred to as First Generation in this book), Second Generation, and Next Generation—and each offers its own set of characteristics, opportunities, and limitations. For the beginner, understanding when and why to use the different types of metal clay may seem a little intimidating, but here's a simple tip to remember: you can't really make a mistake. It's possible to use all the different generations for many different applications. However, certain clay formulas are better suited for different intended uses. If you refer to the following suggestions, you will have successful finished projects. Also, keep in mind, the more you work with this terrific material the less you will have to think about your choices.

First Generation Metal Clay

Characteristics
74% fine silver to 26% binder and water

Metal particles are fluffy like a cotton ball

Metal particles are 20 microns in size

28% shrinkage

Fires at 1650°F (900°C) for 2 hours

Available in clay form

The original formula of metal clay has the longest working time before it dries out and starts cracking. It's perfect for beginners. It carves beautifully in the dry stage, like carving soft wood (see page 42). Also in the dry stage, the material is fairly strong and can be struck with a planishing hammer without breaking due to the higher content of binder in relation to silver. This technique is used in the Forged Link Necklace project on page 116.

Where Does Metal Clay Come From?

You might be wondering, "How is metal clay made?" The process starts with the manufacturing of the pure metal particles that go into the clay. Silver or gold is sprayed (in an atomized form) into a chamber filled with a special kind of gas. The size and shape of the metal particles range from 20 to 5 microns in size, depending on the type of gas used in the chamber.

The next step in the manufacturing process is to collect the powdered metal from the chamber. The silver (or gold) powder is weighed and measured in a laboratory, and then the binder and water are added. After all the ingredients are mixed, the clay is weighed, packaged, and shipped.

The shrinkage of this material is 28 percent. You can use this shrinkage to your advantage. Textures pressed into the moist clay will shrink and appear to become more detailed—think of reducing an image on a copier and the detail seems to become more crisp and clear. Additionally, it's slightly porous, which makes it lighter than conventional fine silver. This is an advantage for designing bigger—but lighter—jewelry pieces.

By using molds it is possible to make matching sets of jewelry, such as a pendant and matching earrings. A mold can be made from Second Generation clay (with 12 percent shrinkage), then First Generation clay can be pressed into the mold. After firing, the piece will be 28 percent smaller than the original. Another amazing trick is to place a layer of the 12-percent-shrinkage clays on top of a slab of First Generation clay. After firing, the piece will "dome up" from the competing shrinkage. The bottom will shrink 28 percent and the top only 12 percent. Experimentation is key to finding ways of making different effects like these.

One disadvantage to using First Generation is its lack of strength in comparison to the other formulas. Because it's slightly more porous, the strength is reduced. It's not the best choice for making rings, cuff bracelets, or toggle clasps. Also, the 28 percent shrinkage can be a challenge to calculate.

Second Generation Metal Clay

Characteristics

90% fine silver to 10% binder and water
Metal particles are perfectly spherical
Metal particles are 5 microns in size
12% shrinkage
Fires at 1650°F (900°C) for at least 10 minutes to 2 hours
Fires at 1560°F (850°C) for at least 20 minutes
Fires at 1470°F (800°C) for at least 30 minutes
Available as clay, slip (paste), syringe, and sheet

One of the biggest advantages to Second Generation metal clay is the lower percentage of shrinkage, only 12 percent. Reducing the shrinkage from 28 percent to 12 percent is a huge difference and is made possible by the lower percentage of binder and water. Because of its spherical-shaped particles, pieces made from Second Generation metal clay are denser and stronger than pieces made from First Generation clay.

This formula offers a range of firing schedules that allows for inclusion materials like pebbles, beach glass, and dichroic glass. The shortest firing time for pieces with no inclusions (stones, glass, etc.) is 10 minutes at 1650°F (900°C). However, for pieces where strength is important (like toggle clasps and rings), you should fire them at 1650°F (900°C) for 2 hours.

far left: Shahasp Valentine
Celechee Necklace #8, 2004
3.4 x 3 x 0.4 cm
Fine silver, 24-karat gold metal clay, fancy
color sapphire; fired in place
Photo by the artist

left: Sherry Cordova
Moorea, 2004
3.8 x 3.3 x 1.2 cm
Recycled bottle glass, coral-imprinted fine
silver metal clay; kiln-fired, coral mold
Photo by Vintage Artifacts

right: Barbara Becker Simon
Green Bead Bracelet, 2001
1.6 x 5.1 x 21.6 cm
Silver metal clay, sterling silver, glass
Photo by Larry Sanders

It's possible to fire some types of glass at the same time you're firing the metal clay. Different glass formulas have different melting temperatures, and experimentation is necessary to determine the best firing schedule for the results you'd like to achieve. For an example of combining glass and Second Generation metal clay, see the Domino Theory earrings on page 76.

The sheet version, originally made for metal clay origami, can also be cut into strips to be used for weaving and braiding. Second Generation clay can be fired for five minutes with a torch, and this shortened firing time can be a significant bonus when time is of the essence.

This version is slightly more expensive than First Generation metal clay. Also, the smaller particles will stick to your hands and tools, so more olive oil hand balm is needed. Since there's less binder than in the First Generation, Second Generation clay tends to dry out rather quickly. However, as you become more experienced, you'll learn ways around this problem. For example, I like working with dry slabs of clay. Once I cut out the shapes, I want the clay to dry quickly. Since this type of clay dries quickly, it's my favorite formula to work with for slab construction.

Next Generation Metal Clay

Characteristics

90% fine silver to 10% binder and water
Metal particles are perfectly spherical
Metal particles are a variety of sizes
12% shrinkage
Fires at 1650°F (900°C) for at least 5 minutes
Fires at 1290°F (700°C) for at least 10 minutes
Fires at 1200°F (650°C) for at least 20 minutes
Fires at 1110°F (600°C) for at least 45 minutes
Available as clay, slip (paste), and syringe

Because this formula has three different sizes of particles, it's the strongest and densest formula (after firing) of all the metal clays. It's by far the best choice for rings, cuff bracelets, and clasps when fired at 1650°F (900°C) for 2 hours. The working properties are more like First Generation metal clay, which makes it more popular with beginners than Second Generation.

This version of metal clay fully sinters (when the pure metal particles bond at high temperature) when fired for 10 minutes at 1290°F (700°C). Next Generation's broad temperature range allows for a wider selection of inclusion materials. Refer to the inclusion materials section on page 52 for a complete list of stones and other items you can use. It's possible to fire sterling silver in with the metal clay at 1110°F (600°C) for 45 minutes. This allows

far left: Aimee Domash
Silver and Gold, 2005
19.1 cm x 2.5 x 1.3 cm
Silver metal clay, sterling silver, gold metal clay; rolled out, pressed, fired, inlay, painted, re-fired, polished, burnished, and assembled
Photo by Don Casper

left: Skylark
Cattails I, 2006
5.5 x 1.7 x 0.5 cm
Silver metal clay, 24-karat gold metal clay
Photo by the artist

for sterling silver pin backs and other sterling silver findings to be fired along with the metal clay, so you can save time by skipping the soldering step. Additionally, Next Generation is the best for torch firing. Once the piece is at temperature, it will completely sinter in only one minute. This immediate gratification is a definite advantage.

The disadvantage to Next Generation metal clay is that it's slightly more expensive. The reason is one of production—to get three different sized metal particles, the production is three times as long as it is for First Generation.

First Generation
24-Karat Gold Metal Clay

Characteristics

85% pure gold to 15% binder and water

Metal particles are fluffy like a cotton ball

Metal particles are 20 microns in size

28% shrinkage

Fires at 1830°F (1000°C) for 2 hours

Available in clay form

There is nothing like 24-karat gold for its shine and luster. Gold metal clay has the same "juicy" working properties as First Generation silver metal clay. Like First Generation silver clay, it carves well and the shrinkage can be used to create exquisite details. Potential disadvantages are its 28 percent shrinkage rate, and its cost. Gold prices vary daily.

Barbara Becker Simon
Marathon Beads 2006
3.2 x 4 cm each
Silver metal clay, 22-karat gold slip, box beads
Photo by Larry Sanders

Ed Biggar
The Fabulous Bat Necklace
Flame-worked glass, metal clay slip
Photo by the artist

Next Generation 22-Karat Gold Metal Clay

Characteristics

Alloy of 91.7% gold 8.3% fine silver with binder and water

Metal particles are perfectly spherical

Metal particles are a variety of sizes

12% shrinkage

Fires at 1650°F (900°C) for at least 10 minutes

Fires at 1560°F (850°C) for at least 30 minutes

Fires at 1380°F (750°C) for at least 60 minutes

Fires at 1290°F (700°C) for at least 90 minutes

Available in clay form

This new type of gold metal clay shrinks the same as Next Generation silver metal clay. This means you can combine it in pieces with Next Generation silver metal clay and fire them together as in the project, Golden Ivy, on page 110. It can also be torch fired with a jeweler's torch.

22-Karat Gold Slip

Characteristics

Alloy of 91.6% pure gold and 8.4% fine silver

Binder provided in a separate bottle

Fires at 850°F (450°C) for 30 minutes in a kiln, and can be fired on a hot plate, by a torch, or in a hot pot mini kiln

This new product, made of 22-karat gold, is used like paint to embellish fired silver pieces. It can be used to decorate specific areas of your design, or you can paint it on to completely cover an object, making it appear as though it's made entirely of solid 22-karat gold. The process creates a layer of gold that's considerably thicker than is possible with electroplating. Using 22-Karat Gold Slip, there's virtually no waste, and a 1-gram package will decorate between 20 and 30 objects. I used this product on the Spiral Galaxy earrings on page 74.

Gold Purchasing Tip

If you are interested in working with gold, it's a good idea to get in the habit of checking the gold market daily. There are online services you can register for that will send you the daily market price on precious metals.

Holly T. Stein
Ginkgo Box, 2003
10.5 x 10.5 x 7.5 cm
Silver metal clay, gingko leaves, brass, sterling silver,
copper, labradonite; hand fabricated, soldered
Photo by Kristen Holub

Forms of Metal Clay

Metal clay comes in several different forms. The most
versatile is Second Generation, which comes as a clay,
slip (also called paste), syringe, and sheet. Each form has
been designed for a specific use. In this section, I'll
describe when and why I use various forms of metal
clay. This isn't a definitive list by any means—there are
new techniques discovered every day by inventive artists
around the world. Perhaps, with a little exploration,
you'll discover a new way to use this incredible material.

Clay

Clay can be rolled out, formed over core materials,
sculpted, or molded to any shape you can imagine.
When it's moist, it will take pressed textures beautifully.
When dry, it can be filed, carved, and details added.

Commercially Prepared Slip (or Paste)

Slip has a higher content of water and more binder than
clay. Use this like glue to attach two dry pieces of metal
clay. Perhaps this is how the term "paste" became associ-
ated with this form of metal clay, because it can be used
to "paste" or glue metal clay pieces together.

I use the commercially prepared slip to cover
organic objects like twigs and sea pods, or to
paint fabric with interesting textures like lace
or burlap. This opens up incredible potential for designing mixed media pieces. For
example, combining fine silver lace with
fused glass has wonderful possibilities.
Another exciting technique is to use the
commercially prepared slip with a rubber
stamp to stamp fine silver onto glass or
enameled surfaces.

**Clockwise from top: metal clay slip, sheet metal clay, lump
metal clay, and metal clay syringe**

right: Debbi Clifford
Dragonfly Glasswing Earrings, 2005
6 x 3 x 0.1 cm each
Silver metal clay, plique-á-jour; syringe-
applied and kiln fired with enamel added
and kiln fired
Photo by Richard Brunck

far right: Terry Kovalcik
Fish, 2005
2.8 x 2 x 1.5 cm
Silver metal clay, silver metal clay sheet;
oxidized, dry construction, cut, and
appliquéd
Photo by Corrin Jacobsen Kovalcik

Syringe

The syringe form of metal clay is slip mixed to the perfect proportions of binder, water, and silver so that it can
be extruded through a syringe-like tool (hence, the
name). I'm often asked by my students if it's possible to
make and load their own syringe. While it is possible,
getting the right consistency takes time and patience. If
you add too much water, the extruded slip collapses into
a puddle, and with too little water it's impossible to push
the mixture out of the syringe. If you're lucky, and hit the
right consistency, then air bubbles are often present,
which create gaps, or blowouts, as you use the syringe.
My suggestion: Save yourself time and trouble, and purchase the ready-to-use syringe.

Syringe can be used to fill joints, adhere dry parts, mend
repairs, or to set stones. It can be extruded as decoration
and used in much the same way as icing is used with a
piping bag in cake decorating. I use the syringe like a
caulking gun to glue together the dry slabs of metal clay
to create simple to elaborate box constructions. If you
won't be using your opened syringe for some time, or
when traveling, place the syringe in a floral vial with
water to keep the clay moist and ready to use.

Sheet

This unique form of metal clay was developed to be
used for the art of origami. The binder is different
from the other forms of metal clay and allows the
sheet to stay flexible for a very long time. I left a piece
unwrapped for one full year just to see what would
happen. After a year, it was still flexible, although a bit
crunchy, and would break if I forced the sheet into too
many folds. Metal clay sheet can be used for weaving,
braiding, or in combination with glass. It will hold an
embossed texture and has a lot of potential for applied
decoration.

CHAPTER 2

Tools, Equipment & Your Workspace

Getting started involves gathering your tools and equipment and setting up your workspace. Metal clay is nontoxic, so you could work at your kitchen table, but you may want to claim a space that you don't have to clean up every night before you eat your supper. I've organized what you need to start working with metal clay. The list may look a bit long, but it's not really, especially when compared to the investment you'd have to make to set up a traditional metal-working studio.

Tools for Working the Clay

You may already have some of these tools around your home, especially if you're involved with any other arts and crafts. Who knows, you may already have everything for the Basic Tool Kit, or even the Deluxe Tool Kit. Complete kits are available from most metal clay suppliers, and specific tools may vary slightly from different distributors.

Basic Tool Kit

The Basic Tool Kit has a great selection of essential tools. It's recommended for beginners because of affordability.

Plastic Rolling Pin

The most economical way to use the lump form of metal clay is to roll it out to a flat sheet, much like rolling out pie dough. For this you'll need some type of plastic rolling pin. I use a piece of PVC pipe available from home improvement centers.

Watercolor Brush

For joining moist clay to moist clay a simple brush of water will do the trick. A watercolor brush is the perfect tool for this task.

Craft Knife

The craft knife is primarily used to cut a moist clay slab into a variety of shapes. I also use the tip of a craft knife to drill holes in bone-dry clay.

Stainless Steel Blade

My friend and colleague, Chris Darway, invented and manufactures a unique cutting tool. It serves a variety of uses. One end of the stainless steel blade has a 90° bend that's useful when building square boxes, and the other end is a 45° angle, perfect for making a mitered seam.

Needle Tool

The needle tool is a basic tool in the ceramic artist's toolbox. It's also known as a pin tool, and I use the names interchangeably. These tools are available through most pottery suppliers. I use the needle tool

Basic tool kit: (from left to right) plastic rolling pin, stainless steel blade, double-ended blender tool, watercolor brush, jeweler's tweezers, burnishing tool, needle tool, wire brush, craft knife.

as a cutting tool, and it's especially useful for cutting out moist clay while using a plastic template because it won't cut the sides of the template like a craft knife will.

Double-Ended Blender Tool

This blender tool can be purchased through pottery suppliers. It's used for sculpting and molding moist clay, blending together seams, and pushing clay, syringe, or slip into cracks for repairs.

Jeweler's Tweezers

It's always handy to have a pair of tweezers around for setting small chips of solder in place when soldering, holding your piece while using patina, or picking up small stones when stone setting.

Brass Wire Brush

The first step in finishing your pieces after firing is to use soap and water with a brass wire brush. This will give the fired metal a soft satin finish.

Burnishing Tool

Use a burnishing tool to achieve a high polish in specific areas on a piece. As opposed to the wire brush, this tool is used dry and rubbed across the surface of the metal. Burnishing tools come in a variety of shapes and sizes and are available through jewelry suppliers or in the printmaking section of art supply stores.

Robert Dancik
Nuts and Bolts of It All, 2006
8.0 x 3.9 x 3.9 cm
Silver metal clay, faux bone, brass nuts
and bolts, sterling silver
Photo by Douglas Foulke

Terry Kovalcik
Triangle Locket, 2005
7 x 1.6 x 1 cm
Silver metal clay, silver metal clay
sheet, sterling silver; oxidized,
dry construction
Photo by the artist

Deluxe Tool Kit

This tool kit was designed with
the intermediate to advanced
metal clay artist in mind.
Many of the tools are the same
as the ones found in the Basic
Tool Kit, but they're often
higher quality for better per-
formance.

Clear Plastic Rolling Pin
Clear plastic is preferred by
many metal clay artists because
you can see through the rolling
pin as you work with the clay.

Tissue Blade
Tissue blades are the same types
of blades used in the medical field
to take cross section tissue samples.
In addition to making precise,
straight cuts, they can be "flexed," or bent, to make
gently curving cuts. You can find them at polymer clay
suppliers, or your favorite craft and hobby shop.

Taper Point Blender Tool
This type of blender tool has a softer, more flexible tip
than the type used in the Basic Tool Kit. They're typically used to blend soft media like oil pastels, paint,

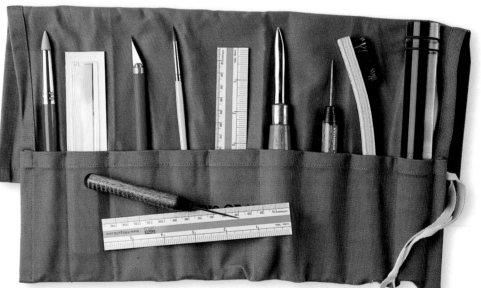

Deluxe tool kit: (from left to right) taper point blender tool,
stainless steel blade, craft knife, watercolor brush, metal clay shrinkage
ruler, burnishing tool, needle tool, brass wire brush, clear rolling pin

and charcoal and can be found in fine
art supply stores.

Metal Clay Shrinkage Ruler
If you're confused by the shrinkage rates of the different
formulas of metal clay, you'll want to own a shrinkage
ruler. This handy tool will help you predict shrinkage
rates. They're available through metal clay suppliers.

Other Necessities

This is a list of other supplies, tools, and equipment you will need to have for making the projects in this book.

Plastic Straws

Make a valuable addition to your toolbox by collecting various sizes of drinking straws. Just by visiting a local convenience store, you can often find different sizes of straws: one for regular soft drinks, one for the jumbo size drinks, one for frozen drinks, and small ones used as coffee stirrers.

Use plastic straws for cutting holes out of moist clay, or use them like a cookie cutter to cut small circle shapes used for decoration.

Emery Boards

In the dry stage, silver clay can be filed with the same emery boards used to file artificial fingernail extensions. Emery boards are also known as salon boards and are widely available. Go ahead and purchase coarse and fine grit types to add to your tool kit. Each side has a different grit so you will have four different grits for sanding and filing the dry metal clay. Emery boards are also available in smaller sizes for getting into hard-to-reach spots.

Plastic Palette Knife

A plastic palette knife is a must for making your own slip (a description for making slip can be found on page 40). Palette knives are available in most art supply stores.

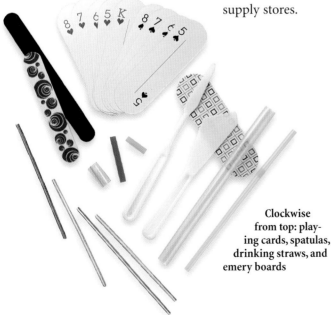

Clockwise from top: playing cards, spatulas, drinking straws, and emery boards

Spacers

When metal clay is fired it shrinks in every direction, even in the thickness. That's why it's important to roll out clay as uniformly as possible. A deck of playing cards is my favorite spacer system. There are other systems available from metal clay suppliers, but I'm happy to stack playing cards to determine how thick my clay slab will be. For pieces made with Second or Next Generation clay, I prefer to roll out the clay to the thickness of three or four playing cards. If I'm making a piece with First Generation clay, I often use mat board, which is equal to four or five playing cards. For pieces that I'd like to carve or water-etch, I'll often use craft sticks, which are roughly equal to eight playing cards in thickness.

Work Surfaces

I use two different work surfaces with metal clay: one rigid, and one flexible. My rigid work surface is a sheet of plate glass that's 18 x 24 inches (45.7 cm x 61 cm), and at least ¼ inch (6 mm) thick. I also have a smaller one to use for rolling out snakes.

I use a nonstick, heat-resistant baking sheet as my flexible work surface. To be productive, I have a stack of nonstick sheets at the ready so I can work on more than one piece at a time.

Various work surfaces: grid paper in a clear presentation sleeve, styrene plastic, vinyl floor tile, nonstick cooking sheet, and a self-healing cutting mat

When I travel or teach classes, I use an 8½ x 11-inch (21.6 cm x 27.9 cm) piece of either styrene plastic or mat board as my rigid work surface, and a clear plastic report cover for the flexible work surface.

Slip Container

An airtight plastic or glass container is perfect for holding your scraps of metal clay. All your crumbs of metal clay can go into your slip container to be used again. For making your own slip, see page 40.

Catherine Davies Paetz
All Lined Up, 2005
3.2 x 4.5 x 2.5 cm
Silver metal clay, 24-karat gold metal clay,
photopolymer plate, patina; kum boo
Photo by the artist

Rubber Block

This is a valuable tool for making fine detail work much simpler and works for you in two ways. By placing the bone-dry metal clay on the edge of a rubber block, you are lifting your piece off your work surface so you will have an easier time accessing the edges when sanding, filing, or drilling. The rubber block also works as a support. By resting work on the block, your holding hand won't get fatigued as quickly.

Using rubber blocks as a brace and guide

Wet Wipes

For cleaning your work surface, tools, and hands, a moist or wet wipe is a must have. The silver trapped in the wipe can be sent to a refiner to be recycled. You can find a list of refiners online. Before you wash your hands, use a wet wipe. You'll prevent silver from literally going down the drain.

Moisture Maintainers

The best consistency of metal clay is what you get directly out of a new package. I call this virgin clay. It has the perfect ratio of water to silver and binder. As soon as a package of metal clay is opened, it's exposed to air and the moisture (water) in the clay body starts to evaporate. However, there are products and tricks that will help slow down evaporation and help to keep your clay moist longer.

Olive Oil, or Olive Oil Hand and Lip Balm

Before you start working, rub your hands, work surface, and tools with a thin layer of olive oil or olive oil hand and lip balm. This coating of olive oil will prevent the metal clay from sticking to your hands and tools, and slows water evaporation from the clay as well.

Brushes

Use the watercolor brush from your tool kit to add water when and where you need it. There are also brushes with built-in reservoirs to hold water. They're sold in the watercolor section of art and craft suppliers. A squeeze of the handle drips water onto the bristles of the brush.

Spray Bottle

I live in a semi-arid climate, so a spray bottle is a necessity for keeping clay moist as I sculpt, mold, or blend seams. I've learned to add a drop of glycerin to my spray bottle so each time I mist the surface of the clay, the glycerin will help to slow the drying time.

Plastic Wrap

An excellent way to keep clay moist as you roll it out is to cover it with a layer of heavy plastic wrap. This technique assures a moist and juicy slab of clay, perfect for pressing in textures. I'll use a piece of plastic food wrap like a tent to keep small pieces of clay moist until I am ready to use them. Plastic food wrap can also be used to tightly wrap and store any unused lumps of clay for the next work session.

Extender

To extend the wet working time of the lump form of metal clay, you may choose to add an extender, which is a solution of glycerin, water, and sometimes a bit of food color to give the mixture color. For optimum results, start with a new, unopened package of silver clay. Open and press a dimple, or well, into the center of the lump of clay. Depending on the silver gram weight, add one to three drops of extender into the depression (one drop per 10 grams of weight). Wrap the clay in plastic and knead the clay until it absorbs the extender. Allow it to sit for a minimum of 30 minutes, or overnight for best results. The glycerin needs time to penetrate between the silver particles via the binder, bond with the water molecules, and thereby slow down evaporation. Metal clay treated in this manner is considered a slow-drying version. When I make boxes, I roll out slabs of clay to be used in the bone-dry state. My goal is to get these slabs to

Clockwise from top: container of olive oil, container of extender, plastic spray bottle, dish, water brushes, homemade humidifier, olive oil balm, plastic wrap, yogurt cup with damp sponge

dry quickly so I can start having fun constructing my barns and silos. For this way of working with metal clay, I don't use extender because I want to speed up the drying process instead of slowing it down.

Homemade Humidifiers

As you work, it's important to keep the clay you're not using moist. One way to prevent it from drying out is to store it in plastic wrap. I realize it's a pain to keep wrapping and unwrapping the plastic wrap, and opening and sealing the packaging. A handy solution is to keep your clay under a homemade humidifier. The idea is to have easy access to your clay without exposing it to air. The most basic version of a humidifier is an inverted plastic cup sprayed with a fine mist of water on the inside.

An inverted clay pot serves as a homemade clay humidifier.

A colleague of mine began using a small terra-cotta flowerpot. She added a sponge tied with a cable tie through the hole in the bottom. After the pot is submerged in water for an hour or more, the walls will stay moist for a long time, making it a great natural humidifier. The trapped moisture will help keep the clay moist and juicy for a long time.

The humidifier works best if your metal clay is on a surface that will also hold moisture, such as a small piece of plastic wrap, nonstick sheet, or the corner of your work surface. A glazed terra-cotta saucer is the perfect partner for the inverted pot because the glazed surface won't suck moisture from the metal clay.

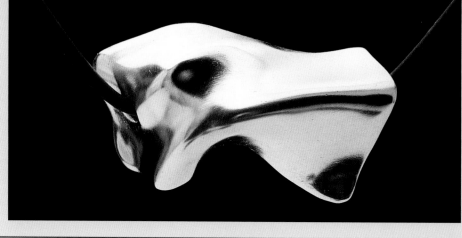

J. Fred Woell
Slice of Life Pendant, 2006
1.9 x 4.4 x 1.3 cm
Silver metal clay
Photo by the artist

Bonus Tools

The more you work with metal clay, the more tools you will acquire. It's human nature. Although I'm a self-proclaimed tool geek myself, I've kept my suggestions here to a minimum.

Carving Tools

The V groove of a carving tool carves into bone-dry metal clay like butter. There are several different brands made specifically for this technique. You can find them in art supply stores in the printmaking section, at fabric and craft shops either with the rubber stamps or with the fine art supplies, and through polymer clay suppliers and some metal clay retailers.

The blades range in durability. Some are made of low-grade tempered steel and will dull quickly, while others are made of higher quality steel and last a long time before getting dull. If you like the carving technique, it will be well worth the investment in higher end carving tools.

Various carving tools

Cutters

An assortment of cutters (from cookie and canapé to special brass cutters with a plunger for easy release) can be used to get quick and precise shapes of metal clay. Cookie and canapé cutters are easy to find in specialty cooking stores, and unusual shapes can be found on the Internet. Brass cutters are found with the polymer clay supplies at craft and hobby stores and from most metal clay suppliers.

Cutters of all shapes and sizes

Additional cutters

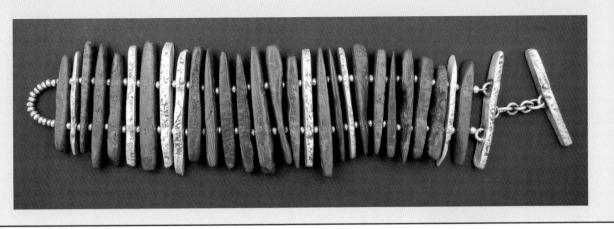

Jean Dixon
Sponge Coral Bracelet,
2006
4.5 x 18.5 cm
Metal clay, sponge coral,
sterling silver
Photo by Hadar Jacobsen

Plastic Templates

If you need to cut out an accurate geometric shape, a pin tool and a plastic template are just the ticket. Plastic templates are sold with drafting tools at office supply or fine art supply stores. When designing by using plastic templates, remember to account for shrinkage depending on which clay formula you are using.

Assorted Blender Tools

Blender tools are available in a variety of sizes and shapes. They also vary in flexibility. Some makers color-code their blending tool tips or handle. The firmest is the black tip, and this type is sold through ceramic and pottery suppliers. The white through dark gray are sold individually or packaged in sets with paintbrushes in fine art supply stores.

Blender tools

Rubber stamps and brass texture sheets provide a variety of ready-made texture patterns.

Texture Tools

Textures can be produced from things found all around you, from the drywall screw in your toolbox, to the bark on the tree in your front yard. In addition, there are several different texture makers that you can purchase. Better yet, why not make your own? Since texture makers work by pressing or rolling out moist clay onto the surface of the texture, you may need to add a thin coating of olive oil to help keep the clay from sticking to the object.

Plastic Texture Sheets

Plastic texture sheets are available from polymer clay suppliers, model train and hobby shops, as well as most metal clay suppliers. There's a wide range of patterns available, and every time I check, they've added more.

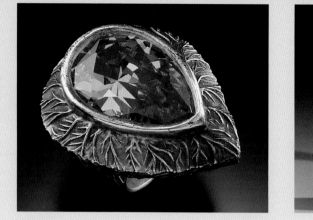

far left: Barbara Becker Simon
Box Ring, 2006
4.4 x 3.8 x 3.8 cm
Silver metal clay, cubic zirconia, 24-karat foil;
box construction
Photo by the artist

left: Susan J. Lewis
It's Good to be Queen Ring, 2004
3.5 x 2.2 x 2.2 cm
Silver metal clay, round amethyst, cubic zirconia, silver black patina; stone-fired in place,
carved, stamped, textured, snake rolled
Photo by Jerry L. Anthony

Full size sheets are 8½ x 11 inches (21.6 x 27.9 cm), and since you only need a quarter of that to work with metal clay, you can cut the sheets with scissors to share with three other friends.

Brass Texture Sheets

Brass texture sheets are strips of sheet brass that have specific textures pressed into them. A standard width is 2½ inches (6.4 cm), but come in a variety of lengths. I recommend starting off with one that's 3 inches (7.6 cm) long.

Rubber Stamps

Rubber stamps are excellent for making a good impression (no pun intended). They're easy to find: fabric stores, craft shops, scrapbook suppliers, and even drug stores carry them. However, if you intend to sell your work, you should know most stamps hold a copyright. Someone created the original artwork for the stamp, and that person gets credit for the design. You should use your own designs or use copyright-free images; other-wise you're infringing on a copyright.

Better yet, you can have your own drawings made into rubber stamps by companies that make business stamps. You provide the drawing made with black ink on plain white paper, and you'll get back your design in relief. Ask for the matrix and die, and you will get a concave and convex version of your original design. I've also made my own rubber stamps by carving plastic erasers with a craft knife.

Homemade Texture Tools

Chances are, you can turn a favorite doodle, sketch, or found texture into a one-of-a-kind texture making tool. Then, by using it in your creative process, you'll give your pieces a distinctive look.

Carving Blocks and Plastic Erasers

Carving blocks are available in the printmaking section of art supply stores. Many brands are available and are usually color coded to specify flexibility, softness, and thickness. Try several types to see which characteristics you prefer.

Carving textures into large art erasers is also an effective way of creating unique designs. Work with bold graphic designs. Avoid trying designs that are intricate or detailed. Draw your design on the surface of the eraser. Remember, straight lines are easier to carve than curved ones. Start by using a carving tool at a shallow angle, increasing the carving angle and depth as you go.

Molds

The most popular mold material for metal clay is a two-part silicone-molding compound. There are many differ-ent varieties, and all work basically the same way. To make a mold, combine equal parts of the two different compounds and knead them together until they mix into one solid color with no marbling or streaks. Press the original object into the soft, putty-like compound. Allow the mold to cure (depending on the brand, this takes anywhere from 5 to 20 minutes). To test whether the compound is set, press a tool into the side of the mold.

Bianca Terranova
Sea Spirals pin, 2006
5.7 x 2.5 x 0.8 cm
Silver metal clay, brass,
copper, nickel, ammonite;
hand fabricated
Photo by the artist

Assorted silicone molds

If the tool leaves an impression, the compound needs more time. After the mold cures, you can remove the object from the mold. Silicone molds are naturally slick, so you won't need to use olive oil to get the clay to release from the mold.

Polymer Clay Plates and Molds

Polymer clay is versatile for making a plethora of textures because it can be used to make texture plates or as a mold material. To make a texture plate from polymer clay, roll out a slab of polymer and cure by following the manufacturer's instructions. It's worth investing in a reliable oven thermometer so you properly cure the polymer. When the slab cools, it can be carved with the same carving tools used to carve plastic erasers, or metal clay. The best type of polymer clay to use as a texture maker is the one that remains flexible after baking so the metal clay will release easily. A light layer of olive oil will help.

Drying Equipment

Before firing metal clay, it's important to make sure the piece is completely dry, also known as bone dry. Moisture remaining in the clay could turn to steam and cause a rip, tear, or blister as it finds an escape route out of your piece. These mishaps can be repaired. However, if you fire your metal clay when it's fully dry, you probably won't need to make repairs.

Letting your pieces air dry is always an option. However, if you live in a humid climate, you may have to leave your work out for an extended period time to dry fully. To speed up the process, you can use a number of devices such as a hair dryer, a heat gun, or a food dehydrator. You can also place pieces on top of a hot kiln to dry, or even under a hot lamp.

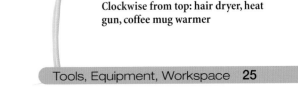

Clockwise from top: hair dryer, heat gun, coffee mug warmer

In some cases, kilns can be programmed to hold a low temperature of 250°F (121°C), perfect for drying metal clay.

Food dehydrators are especially good to use for drying metal clay. Since they circulate air on all sides of a piece, the clay will dry flat and not warp.

Personally, I use a coffee mug warmer because it's small and portable.

How Dry?

To test to see if the clay still has moisture, you'll need a mirror or a shiny piece of tin, like the lid to a mint box. Place the piece on the mirror or tin for three seconds, remove the piece, and if there is a fog on the surface, the clay is still wet. If the piece is still wet, use one of the methods listed to completely dry the metal clay.

Firing Tools and Supplies

There are several different options for firing metal clay as well as supplies to use with the different heating sources. In addition to a way to fire your work, you will need firing tools, kiln furniture, and support material.

Heat Sources

To fire metal clay you need something that will reliably heat the silver or gold to its required sintering temperature. This section will give you an overview of your options, and explain some advantages and disadvantages. If you're just getting started, you may want to use a less expensive alternative, such as a butane torch, hot pot, or trinket kiln. The best option is to use a metal clay kiln because they're designed especially for firing this amazing material.

Torches

Second and Next Generation metal clay can be fired with a torch. Next Generation will sinter with a torch if you keep the color of the metal clay between bright pink and dull red for one minute. For Second Generation, you

Two styles of butane torches

need to hold the metal clay between bright pink and dull red fire for five minutes. While it's technically possible to fire First Generation with a torch, it isn't practical because you would need to hold the torch for two hours.

Different torches are designed to be used with different types of gas. Butane, propane, and acetylene will get hot enough to properly sinter metal clay. As a matter of fact, each will get hot enough to melt the pieces, so it is recommended to first practice firing with a torch to get comfortable with the process.

Butane

Small handheld butane torches are available at hardware and gourmet cooking stores. They're inexpensive, portable, and refillable. They can also be used for small soldering applications.

right: Susan J. Lewis
Inro Box, 2006
5 x 5 x 3 cm (box), 6.6 cm (necklace)
Silver metal clay, synthetics, ojime
bead, silver metal clay tubing, tube
bead, end caps, silver black patina;
stamped, hollow constructed.
Photo by Jerry L. Anthony

far right: Linda Kaye-Moses
Vento di Est; Katrina, 2006
10 x 7 x 0.5 cm
Fine silver, sterling silver, 14-karat gold
metal clay, enamel, pearl
Photo by Evan J. Soldinger

Acetylene

An acetylene/atmospheric air system is a type of torch setup used for traditional metalsmithing applications such as annealing, soldering, and light casting. This system can be used to torch-fire metal clay. Acetylene is very accessible, reasonably priced, and creates a hot, concentrated flame.

Propane

A propane/oxygen system is another set up used by traditional metalsmiths for annealing, soldering, light casting, and can be used to fire metal clay. The system includes

An acetylene torch

propane tank and regulator, oxygen tank and regulator, two sets of hoses, and a torch handle with interchangeable tips. Propane tanks can be exchanged at grocery stores, gas stations, and hardware stores, so it's more accessible than acetylene. Bottled oxygen will last for a long time and can be filled (also purchased) at your local bottled gas company. Reasonable cost and a clean-burning flame make propane a good choice for metalsmiths.

Hot Pot

There are two versions of this firing system. The big differences are in price and durability. One is ceramic and the other is made of a composite fiber, and both work equally well for firing Next Generation metal clay. The fuel is alcohol based, and is similar to the type used under a fondue pot. The hot pot is a good choice for beginners who aren't sure they're ready to make the investment in a kiln. Advantages to the hot pot are that it's extremely portable and works well for fusing 22-karat gold slip. Limitations are the small number of pieces that can be fired on the 3-inch (7.6 cm) diameter screen, and that it can only be used to fire Next Generation metal clay.

Speed Fire Cone System

The latest innovation for firing metal clay is a propane-fueled firing system called a speed fire cone. It's made of a composite fiber with a metal screen on top. This system offers an accurate pyrometer (a device that displays the temperature), so it provides enough flexibility to fire all metal clay formulas and for enameling pieces. Propane cylinders are readily available in many retail stores, and come in a variety of

Speed fire cone system

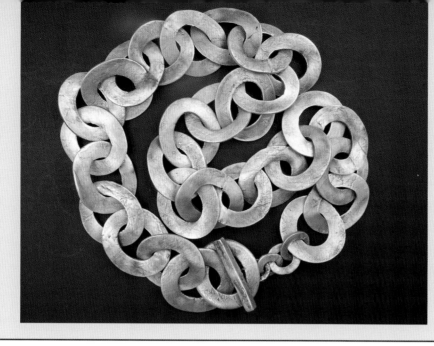

Jean Dixon
Chain Necklace, 2005
2.5 x 47 cm
Silver metal clay
Photo by Hadar Jacobsen

sizes. Additionally, with the purchase of the bulk adapter, it can be attached to a standard tank (such as the type used for barbecue grills). However, a limiting factor is the number of pieces that can be fired on the 4-inch (10.2 cm) diameter screen. The speed fire cone system is available online through some metal clay suppliers.

Trinket Kiln

This small, electronic kiln can be used to fire small pieces, as an enameling kiln, and is an excellent heat source for kum boo when used with brass plate inserts. It's small, compact, and lightweight, making it extremely portable. One disadvantage is that the size limits the number of metal clay pieces you can fire at once.

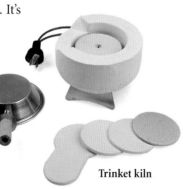

Trinket kiln

Metal Clay Kilns

There are two manufacturers in the United States that produce kilns for firing metal clay. The latest versions have five preprogrammed firing schedules, and one you can program yourself. These kilns plug into a regular three-prong outlet and will monitor the temperature and time. Ceramic or glass kilns aren't recommended because they have hot spots that could melt metal clay.

Using a metal clay kiln allows you to fire multiple pieces at one time; you can stack as many as three kiln shelves per firing. As you're running a firing cycle, you can busily prepare another, so your production dramatically increases. These units can be pricey, but it's well worth the investment if you're a metal clay maniac. Kilns can be purchased through most metal clay suppliers and special ordered with wiring for any country.

A metal clay kiln

Firing Tools

You will need additional tools when working with metal as hot as 1650°F (900°C): a long-handled spatula, kiln fork, long tweezers, heat-resistant gloves, hot pads or trivets, and a digital kitchen timer.

Spatula

The long-handled type of spatula used for outdoor grilling works great for unloading hot shelves from the kiln. The type with a clamp is my new favorite.

Kiln Fork

These tools are designed for enameling, and should be used with heat-resistant gloves to place and remove enamel work from a hot kiln. They're available from enamel suppliers.

Gloves

Heat-resistant gloves are important. I have several types for different uses. For kum boo and 22-karat gold slip, a light-duty workman's leather glove from the hardware store works well to fend off the heat of a hot plate or trinket kiln. For enameling or unloading from a hot kiln, you'll want a heavy-duty heat-resistant glove made of a non-asbestos material. These are available through jewelry suppliers.

Hot Pads / Trivets

You need a heat-resistant surface to place hot shelves onto when unloading the kiln. I have a large slab of slate next to my kiln, but a solder pad or kitchen trivet will do the job.

Kitchen Timer

A digital kitchen timer is an especially useful tool when torch firing or enameling. It will remind you when to remove your piece from the heat to avoid disaster.

Clockwise from top: heat-resistant gloves, kiln forks, grill spatula, firing pad, timer

Kiln Furniture

Anything that stays in the kiln during firing is known as kiln furniture; not tables and chairs, but shelves, props, spacers, and blocks. Ceramic kiln suppliers have a wide assortment of kiln furniture made to last over years of firing. A less expensive alternative is to use solder pads, which are available through jewelry suppliers. Although these will crack and break, the pieces are still useable. You can stack three shelves high in one firing as long as the top shelf isn't higher than the thermocouple (a probe in the kiln chamber that measures the temperature). Heat rises and the space above the thermocouple is hotter than the pyrometer reading. Fine silver has a melting temperature of 1762°F (961°C). Metal clay pieces that reach this temperature will melt.

Kiln furniture: shelves, blocks, and spacers

Support Material

When firing a three-dimensional object (spheres, cubes, pyramids, etc.), you'll need to engineer a way to support it during the firing or it will slump and change shape. For example, if a spherical bead were fired flat on a kiln shelf with no support, it would come from the kiln with a flat spot on the bottom. To support three-dimensional objects, it's best to bury the piece halfway in a support material such as vermiculite, pearlite, or kitty litter.

You'll need something to hold this loose material, such as a terra-cotta flowerpot saucer, steel ring, or you can build a box with kiln shelves to hold the loose material and your piece. If you're firing an unusual shape, there is a type of paper clay that can be used as a prop and will survive the firing because the main ingredient is volcanic ash.

Vermiculite support material in a terra-cotta saucer

Vermiculite

Vermiculite is mica and is found in large bags anywhere garden supplies are sold. In gardening, it's used to mix into dense soil. Either pearlite or kitty litter can be used as a substitute.

Pearlite

Pearlite is ground pumice and works great as a support material. Pumice comes *from* volcanoes, so it won't have any problem withstanding any of the metal clay firing temperatures.

Cat Litter

Cat litter can be used as a support material, but only use a brand without additives. Pure clay can handle the different firing temperatures and schedules, and is easy to find at grocery stores. Use it in a terra-cotta saucer to create an inexpensive firing solution for beads and other three-dimensional objects.

Alumina Hydrate

Alumina hydrate is a fine white powder that is a byproduct of aluminum refining. It can be used as a support material or by sprinkling a fine dusting (less than $\frac{1}{16}$ inch [1.6 mm]) on your kiln shelf when firing a band ring. The fine powder acts like miniature ball bearings to allow for even shrinkage. Be warned, alumina hydrate is a known carcinogen. Always wear a dust mask and respirator when handling it, and wash your hands thoroughly after using it. For this reason, I seldom use alumina hydrate except for firing band rings. It can be purchased through metal clay and ceramic suppliers.

Paper Clay

One type of paper clay—made of volcanic ash, talc, water, starch, and wood pulp—works well as a firing support. It's simple to shape, air hardens, and can be used in multiple firings. It's available at craft and hobby shops in the polymer clay aisle, or in fine art supply stores with the modeling clays.

Specialty Tools

One of my goals in this book is to broaden the way in which artists work with metal clay. Combining other materials with metal clay has exciting potential. To work with enamel, glass, and nonferrous metals, you will need tools and supplies specific for these media.

Flexible Shaft Tool

When you decide to make a serious commitment to working with metal, you'll benefit greatly from the help of a flexible shaft tool. It's basically a motor with a flexible shaft and a hand piece. The chuck in the hand piece will accept different tools for a wide variety of techniques: drilling, cutting, sanding, grinding, and polishing. Hobby grades are available at hardware stores or craft and hobby shops. Professional to industrial grades are available through jewelry suppliers.

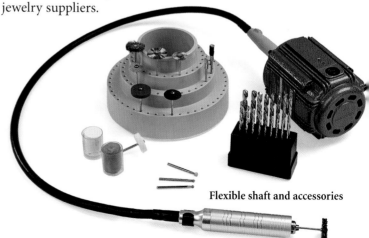

Flexible shaft and accessories

Barbara Becker Simon
Collage I, 2005
48.3 x 2.5 cm
Stainless steel, silver metal
clay, granite, glass; box beads
Photo by Larry Sanders

Flexible Shaft Accessories

Drill bits, cutting burs, sanding discs, grinding wheels, steel and brass brushes, mini felt, and cloth buffing wheels are made to fit in the hand piece of a flexible shaft. Accessories are designed to replace the labor-intensive work traditionally done by hand. However, before you start, I highly recommend you practice and learn how to control a motorized tool.

Using the flexible shaft tool and a wire brush to finish a surface

Shaping Tools

After your metal clay pieces are fired, they can be bent and shaped in the same ways metalsmiths form copper, sterling, brass, or gold to make rings or bracelets. You can shape flat-fired pieces with a rawhide or rubber mallet and bracelet or ring mandrel. Don't use a metal hammer for this technique because metal will leave a mark on the fine silver.

Tools for shaping metal: (from left to right) ring mandrel, rawhide mallet, bracelet/cuff mandrel

Enameling Tools and Supplies

In addition to powdered enamel, you will need the following: sifter, holding agent (also known as gum binder or gum tragacanth), tweezers, plastic spoon, watercolor brush, plastic watercolor paint tray, and small clear glass or plastic containers with tight-fitting lids. Tools for firing the enamel are a kiln, kiln fork, digital timer, steel trivet, and screen.

Enameling tools and supplies: (clockwise from top) sifters, enamel powder and binding agent, watercolor paint tray, tweezers, watercolor brush, plastic spoon, watercolor tray, and various plastic containers; (center) mesh firing platform, and firing trivet

Soldering Tools and Supplies

The bare basics for soldering are a torch, silver solder, paste flux, flux brush, solder pad, tweezers, and slow cooker with a pickle solution of sodium bisulphate.

Soldering is a skill that anyone can learn. If you can't take a class, books and videos are readily available on the subject. Soldering equipment and supplies are available through jewelry suppliers.

Soldering tools and accessories: (from top to bottom) butane torch, paste flux, locking tweezers, solder, and labeled plastic containers

Glass Tools and Supplies

To cut sheet glass you will need a glass cutter, glass cutting oil, metal cork backed ruler, running pliers, breaking pliers (also called grozing pliers), and protective gloves and goggles. After donning your gloves and goggles, dip the glass cutter in the oil. Place the ruler on the glass and run the glass cutter along the ruler, pressing down firmly. This will score the glass. You should hear a "zipping" sound as you score the glass. Lift the glass and use the running pliers to snap off the piece. Breaking pliers are for breaking off smaller pieces that are too small for the running pliers. If your piece is not cut perfectly, don't fret; you'll get better with time. It is a good idea to practice on inexpensive window glass until you get the

hang of glass cutting. Typically, glass cutting supplies can be found at the hardware store. Top-of-the-line glass cutting tools are available at craft and hobby shops, stained glass shops, or online.

Finishing Tools and Supplies

Once your piece is fired, the metal can be given a variety of finishes: satin, high polish, mirror finish, or some combination of each. You can achieve these finishes by using wire brushes, burnishing tools, sandpaper, needle files, polishing cloths, and a tumbler with stainless steel shot and burnishing compound.

Various finishing tools: (clockwise from top) polishing paper, polishing cloth, burnishing tools, assorted wire brushes

Glass cutting tools: (from left to right) goggles, running pliers, permanent marker, glass cutter, and ruler

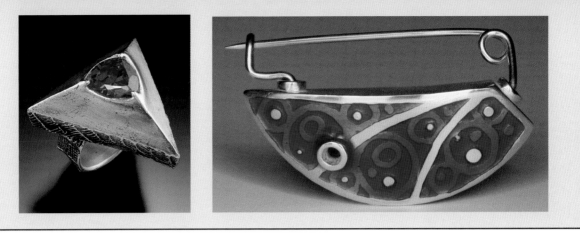

right: Barbara Becker Simon
Box Rings, 2006
4.4 x 3.8 x 3.8 cm
Silver metal clay, cubic zirconia,
24-karat foil; box construction
Photo by the artist

far right: Catherine Davies Paetz
Into the Blue, 2006
3.2 x 5.1 x 1.3 cm
Silver metal clay, enamel, sterling
silver; water-etched, hollow formed
Photo by the artist

Workspace

Metal clay benefits from being extremely portable. I have heard of metal clay artists working on a space as small as a tray table on an airplane as they traveled, or as remote as a picnic table at the top of Pike's Peak.

I'm extremely lucky to have a supportive spouse and a space all to myself for my creative endeavors. My studio is a converted one-car garage, and I work at a long bench that measures 8 x 2½ feet (2.4 m x 76.2 cm)(see photo below).

At each end of the bench I have secured an adjustable-arm desk lamp fitted with a 100-watt bulb. As my eyes age, I require more light to see fine detail clearly. Therefore, in addition to the desk lamps I have a small, natural-light flip lamp I move to exactly where I need more light.

I park myself on an office chair on wheels so I can roll back and forth from one station to another as needed. I just have to be careful not to run over one of my cats that like to keep me company in the studio. For hammering and shaping metal, I found an old butcher-block workbench. It's sturdy and works well for heavy-duty work.

For enameling, I prefer to stand at a tall drafting table that is easier to keep clean and is on the opposite end of the studio far away from the dust and dirt that accumulates on my workbench. I keep my kiln on a metal rolling cart that has one shelf to store all my firing supplies. If I'm ever firing something that produces a lot of smoke, such as twigs, cork clay, or wax, I can roll the kiln and the whole works outside.

Once you have decided which project to start with, you can get all your tools and supplies together and get busy. Most importantly, remember to have fun!

Organized left to right: flex shaft and accessories, dry metal clay working area, wet metal clay working area, mugs and jars of tools, and soldering area with pickle pot and rinse water.
Photo by Craig DeMartino

CHAPTER 3

Making It with Metal Clay

Now that you've selected a type of metal clay, gathered your tools and equipment, and set up your workspace, it's time to get busy making new and wonderfully creative things. I've organized this chapter in a sequential manner. I'll cover working wet, various drying methods, working dry, and firing options with a bonus tutorial on how to torch fire metal clay. The section on post-firing techniques includes finishing options, as well as the use of liver of sulfur patina. This section gives you all the information you need to complete your metal clay pieces with style.

Whenever possible, I have included helpful tips for working with this amazing material. Beginners may feel intimidated, but metal clay is very forgiving. You can't go wrong, so have fun.

Keeping Clay Moist and Other Tricks of the Trade

Metal clay that's fresh from the manufacturers packaging is the perfect clay—it's got the exact balance of moisture. When you squish it between your thumb and index finger, there are no cracks in the clay body (see photo 1). However, as soon as you start handling it, it begins to lose moisture. When your metal clay dries out, you can bring it back to life.

You'll find numerous tools and tricks for keeping metal clay moist listed under Maintaining Moisture on page 20, but first, you need to understand the different stages of dryness.

Slightly Dry

Metal clay is considered slightly dry when you squish a pea-sized ball of clay between your thumb and index finger and small cracks form at the edges (see photo 2). This clay needs a little moisture. Add a fine mist of water to the clay and knead it between plastic wrap. By kneading between plastic, you will keep the clay from further drying out and keep your fingers clean.

After kneading water into the clay, wrap the clay tightly and allow it to sit for at least 10 minutes. This gives the water particles time to seep in between the particles of silver via the binder. Giving rehydration enough time is an essential step to having the perfect working consistency of metal clay. Don't rush the process!

Mostly Dry

If the clay is mostly dry, it's hard to pinch between your fingers (see photo 3). It will crumble or crack apart because most of the water has evaporated. This clay can be rehydrated, but it will take time and patience. First, place the clay in an airtight container and poke the lump a few times with the wooden end of a paintbrush to create a surface with many small holes. Next, add enough water to fill all the holes. Allow the water to be fully absorbed by the clay; this could take a few hours or a few days depending on the condition of the clay. When the water is absorbed, knead the clay between plastic wrap and add more water as needed. When you have reached a consistency that is similar to a brand new package of metal clay, wrap it tightly in plastic wrap and allow it to sit overnight. The next morning you will have moist and juicy clay.

Bone Dry

If the clay is bone dry it will need to be ground into dust. To rehydrate, use the coarse emery file to grind the clay into a fine powder. Sweep the dust into an airtight container and add only enough water to cover the particles and set it aside for several days. When the water has been completely absorbed, use a plastic pallet knife to transfer the slurry onto some plastic wrap. It will be a sticky mess. Alternate kneading the clay between the plastic wrap and opening it up to the air to dry. Eventually, the clay will become close to its original consistency. When this point is reached, wrap it tightly and (you guessed it) allow it to sit overnight. This is a very economical way of reclaiming or recycling your metal clay.

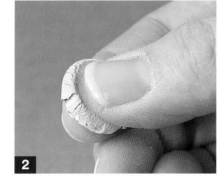
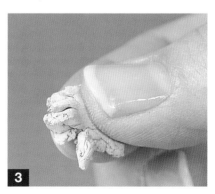

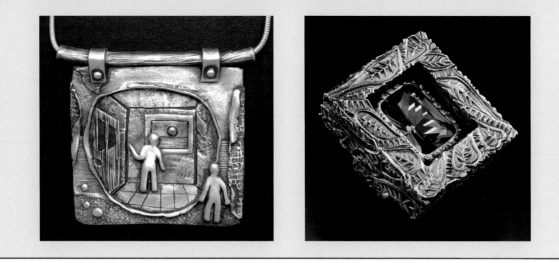

far left: **Hadar Jacobsen**
Multiple Exposures, 2005
5.1 x 5.1 cm
Silver metal clay, bronze
Photo by artist

left: **Barbara Becker Simon**
Picture Frame Ring, 2006
5.1 x 5.1 x 5.1 cm
Silver metal clay, kum boo,
cubic zirconia
Photo by Larry Sanders

Working Wet

I've found working with wet (moist) metal clay to be a challenge. I don't have the hand skills for working with a squishy material, so I do the minimal amount of work needed and then force dry the clay to bone dry.

However, there is nothing like moist clay for certain techniques such as cutting, texturing, molding, and sculpting.

Rolling Flat

The most economical use of lump material is to roll a slab of clay. (I can get six pairs of earrings from one 28-gram package of metal clay.) To roll out a flat slab, start with the clay directly from the package. Place your choice of spacers (stacked playing cards) on either side of the clay to the desired thickness (see photos 4 and 5). With First Generation clay, I typically use four or five playing cards because of the 28-percent shrinkage. For Second and Next Generation clay, I step it down to two or three playing cards. Take a lightly oiled rolling pin, and roll out the clay between the spacers to make a metal clay slab. The process is like rolling out pie crust. You can also roll out the clay on top of a textured surface and lay a different texture on top to create a two-sided texture.

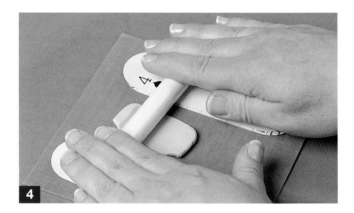

4

5

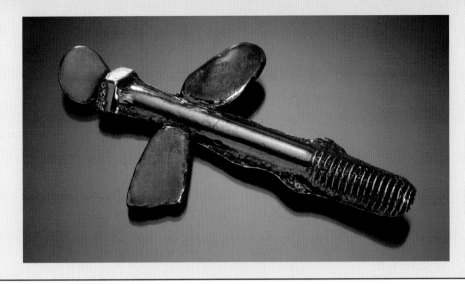

right: **Tim McCreight**
Untitled, 2006
8 x 4 x 1 cm
Fine silver, beach glass
Photo by Robert Diamante

Cutting Shapes

Once the material is rolled out, you can cut out any shape you desire. Using a pin tool and plastic drawing template, you can cut out a wide variety of geometric shapes in a variety of sizes (see photo 6). A craft knife works well for cutting shapes freehand, and a tissue blade or stainless steel blade is great for cutting long straight lines. An assortment of commercially made cutters will add to your repertoire of shapes to use in your metal clay designs (see photo 7).

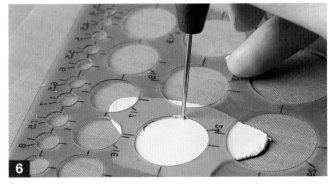

Making Holes and Balls

When the clay is moist, it's very easy to cut holes to attach ear wires, jump rings, or a place to thread a cord or chain. I keep a variety of plastic beverage straws handy for this purpose. Simply use the straw like a cookie cutter, and cut a hole in the metal clay.

If you need to make a bunch of balls of clay exactly the same size, roll out a slab of clay to any thickness, use a straw like a cookie cutter to cut multiple circles of clay, and then roll each disk into a sphere (see photo 8). You can make as many as you need and they will be exactly the same size because you are starting with exactly the same amount of material.

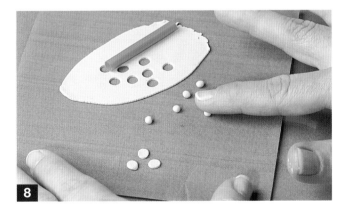

Hadar Jacobsen
Untitled, 2006
3 x 11 x .2 cm
Silver metal clay, copper washers, brass washers; etched, hammered, textured, fired in one piece
Photo by artist

Embossing Texture

The first time you push something into clay to create a textured surface, you'll start seeing the world differently. You'll start noticing interesting textures everywhere you look.

I once called a class into the bathroom because the wall tile had an exceptional textured surface. Look for things with interesting textures at flea markets, thrift stores, toy stores, and hardware stores. I found a treasure trove of things in the kitchen to push into clay for texture: plastic mesh vegetable bags, plastic beverage caps, and even a bamboo sushi roller.

Organic materials like seashells, seedpods, cornhusks, or tree bark create elegant textures I'm drawn to time and again in my work (see photo 9). Hardware stores are a great source for texture-rich items—heads of nuts, bolts, and screws, and there's a world of items in all those little bins.

By repeatedly stamping the clay with a rubber stamp, you can create an interesting overlapping texture (see photo 10). You can also fashion your own texture tools by altering plastic erasers, craft sticks, barbecue skewers, plastic beverage stirrers, etc. In my texture toolbox, I keep small pieces of fabric, like burlap and lace. Fabric can be pushed into the surface of the moist clay, allowed to dry in place, and then fired to capture the most detail.

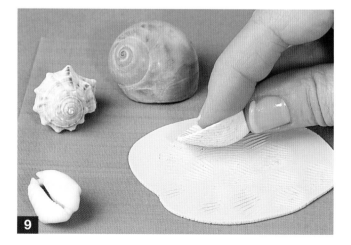

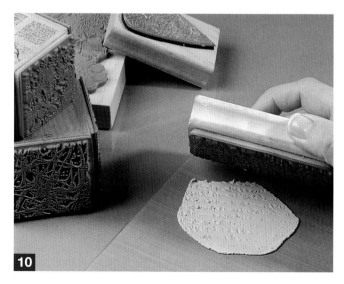

Pressing into Molds

Commercially made molds are available in the candy making section and the polymer clay section of many craft and hobby shops. They are convenient and ready to use, but I find the designs limiting. For those who may be a bit more adventurous, it's possible to make your own molds. You can find more on this on page 24.

To press metal clay into a mold, ball up the moist clay. With the tip of your fingers shape one end of the ball to create a conical shape. The ball of clay now looks like an egg. Press the tip of the egg into the center of the mold and use a flat surface (like a clear plastic lid) to press the clay into the mold. The plastic lid will equalize the pressure on the clay. You can watch as it spreads out to the edges of the mold. Using an egg shape will avoid the chance of capturing air bubbles because it spreads from the center outward.

Mold Making Tip

Use a fine mist of olive oil to coat the inside of the mold before pressing in the metal clay. The oil will make it easier to release the metal clay from the mold. Silicone molds don't need to be coated with olive oil, as the surface of the silicone is naturally slick and the metal clay releases easily. To capture the most detail let the metal clay dry in the mold before removing it.

Sculpting

The main building blocks for sculpting are logs (thick rods of clay), snakes (long, round strands of clay), or peas (small balls of clay).

There is an easy trick for making snakes. You'll need a glass plate surface, and a smaller, 4 x 9-inch (10.2 x 22.9 cm) piece of plate glass or plastic container lid to use as a roller. Start by rolling a coil of metal clay with your finger on the plate glass work surface. Using the lid, roll out the coil of clay (see photos 11 and 12). The roller will help distribute equal pressure to make a uniform

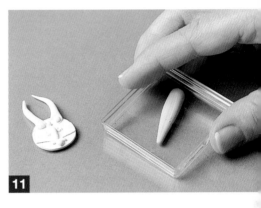

coil. If the clay is cracking as you roll it out, it's too dry and you'll need to add water, knead the clay between plastic wrap, and allow it to sit for 10 minutes before attempting to roll it out again.

To sculpt with these building forms, you'll need to add moist clay to moist clay. Simply apply a brush of water on the two surfaces you wish to attach. Allow the water to penetrate for a few seconds, then lightly press the two pieces together. If one of the pieces is smaller than the other, you can set the smaller piece on the larger one, lightly press together, and brush the perimeter of the smaller piece with water. The water will seep under the seam. Wait a few moments, then check to see if the piece is completely attached. If it has pulled away at the joint, lightly press down and add more water.

Homemade Slip

You can make your own slip and mix it to any consistency you need. Start by taking a pea-size piece of lump clay. Smash the pea on a plastic or glass work surface and add a mist of water from a spray bottle (see photo 13). Use a plastic spatula to force the water into the clay in a smashing motion (see photo 14). Keep working water into the clay until it becomes slick (see photo 15). Place this mixture in an airtight container and add scraps of the same metal clay formula to this slip jar. I keep one jar of slip made of First Generation and another that combines Second and Next Generation because they share the same shrinkage (don't forget to label your slip containers).

Most metal clay artists will keep slip on hand for repairing metal clay pieces before firing. Apply it with a watercolor brush or plastic spatula to fill cracks or glue together breaks.

Wet Repairs

Repairs can be made in moist clay by adding more clay and using a blender tool to smooth the seam (see photos 16 and 17). Don't use water alone to repair a break in the material; it won't work. Depending on how much time you've invested in the piece, it's sometimes a better decision to ball up the clay and start again. Chances are, you'll make a better piece than the original.

Slip Tip

You may want to use distilled water if your tap water is heavy with minerals. I have also learned from potters to add a drop of vinegar to the slip to prevent mold from growing on the organic binder. You can still use moldy slip, but it looks and smells funky.

Drying Methods

There are two approaches to drying metal clay: air drying and forced drying. Air drying takes time—typically pieces are allowed to sit overnight.

Air Dry

If you're working with a thick piece of clay (4 mm or more), it's best to use the air-dry method. Thick pieces need time for the moisture in the center to evaporate naturally. If you force dry thick clay, it tends to crack. Thick pieces are also prime candidates for blisters, so letting the piece dry overnight (preferably up to 24 hours) is best.

Force Dry

To force dry clay, you can use any number of gadgets that will either move air, heat from above, heat from below, or use surrounding heat. Some of the more easy-to-find tools are hair dryers, heat guns, and fruit dehydrators.

Hot Tip

Remember to use tweezers to take the piece off the coffee mug warmer and allow it to cool before touching. I can't tell you how many times I've burned my fingers.

Working Dry

You can do some things with dry metal clay that you can't do (or at least it's very hard to do) when it's wet. With bone dry clay, you can do a lot of fussy detail work, and really obsess over it. Because I come from a traditional metalworking background, I have a "heavy hand" and find I love working the clay in the bone-dry stage.

Refining Edges

When the piece is bone dry, the edges can be refined by filing with emery boards (see photo 18), jeweler's needle files, or carving with a craft knife. When filing, use the coarse emery board first, and then follow with the fine one for a smooth edge. Jeweler's needle files are great for getting into hard-to-reach spots (see photo 19). Try placing the work on a rubber block to raise the piece off the work surface. This will help in the refining step. Carving the sides with a craft knife creates an interesting textured edge, as well.

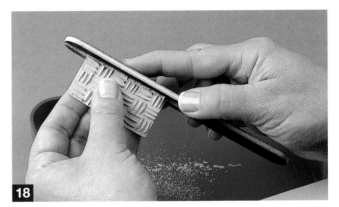

18

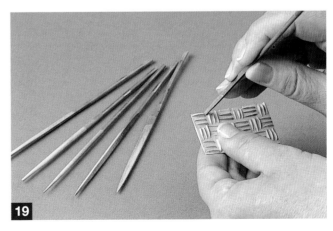

19

Barbara Becker Simon
Big Links, 2006
53.3 x 2.5 cm
Silver metal clay, sterling silver,
stainless steel; hollowed,
embedded, fired
Photo by Larry Sanders

Making Holes

You can drill a hole in the bone-dry clay using the sharp end of a craft knife. Place the piece flat on your work surface, center the tip in the spot where you want a hole, and twist in a drilling motion (see photo 20). When you cut through to the other side, flip the piece and repeat. This is the way I create holes in all my pieces because of the crisp detail.

Carving

For carving, First Generation clay is generally preferred because it carves smoothly. However, it is possible to carve the other formulas of metal clay. The Cuff Style Bracelet on page 107 is carved from Next Generation metal clay.

Carving Metal Clay

1 Select a carving tool with a size No. 1, V-tip. Start with a shallow 22° angle, and begin carving away only a small amount of material (see photo 21). Begin in the center of your design and carve toward the edge. Ease the pressure as you get close to an edge or you could crack the piece.

2 Increase the angle to 45° and carve away more material (see photo 22). If you'd like a deeper cut, change the blade size. It's not recommended to make more than two passes at the 45° angle or you'll risk carving through the piece. If you do break through to the other side, all is not lost. You can add another layer (two playing cards thick) to the back, and when dry, continue carving.

Slab Construction

This is my favorite way of working with metal clay. Slab construction is used to make boxes, so it is also known as box construction.

1 Make a template using pieces of cardstock. Check the proportions and make any changes needed in the design. Once the design is set, the cardstock pieces can be used as the pattern.

2 Roll out a slab of clay four or five playing cards in thickness. After the walls are constructed, the piece will need a lot of sanding. This thickness assures you won't sand through the piece.

3 Place the template pieces on the clay slab, and cut out all the parts.

4 When the slabs are bone dry, glue them together with the metal clay syringe (see photos 24 and 25).

5 Set the piece on a hot plate and wait for the syringe to dry.

6 Use the syringe like a caulking gun to run the material on all the inside seams (see photo 26). Use a blending tool to push the clay into the seams (see photos 27 and 28).

7 Set the piece aside to dry. If any seams are open from the outside, use the syringe to fill the gaps. After the piece is totally dry, sand the edges for a crisp, clean, expertly constructed form.

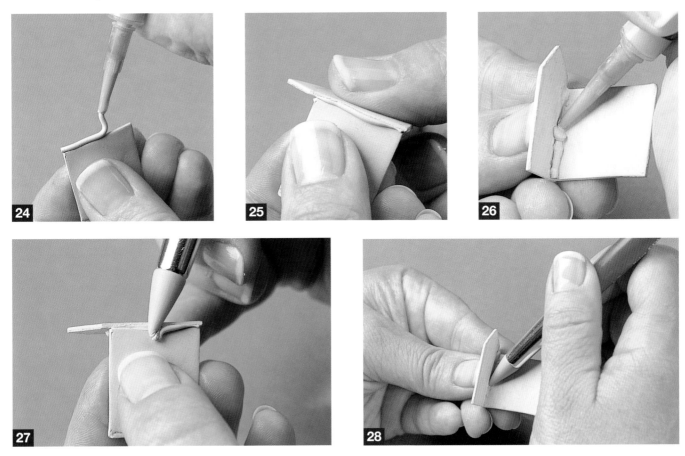

far left: Lorena Lazard
Today We Bury You, 2005
12 x 5 x 3 cm
Sterling silver, silver metal clay,
14-karat gold metal clay, epoxy color,
soil, acrylic
Photo by Paolo Gori

left: Alice Alper-Rein
Color Your World Kaleidoscope and Stand, 2005
9 x 2.5 cm
Silver metal clay, brass, sterling silver,
optical lens, front surface mirror
Photo by artist

Dry Repairs

In the dry stage of metal clay, cracks can be repaired with thick slip or with a snake of moist clay. Breaks can be glued back together with the syringe.

With Slip

To repair a small crack with thick slip, brush water on the crack and let it soak into the clay. It will take a moment for the water to activate the binder; the area will get slightly moist and sticky. Apply thick slip with a plastic pallet knife and work it down into the crack with a blender tool. If you go across the crack, not down the crack, you will fill the gap more efficiently. To repair a large crack, more clay is needed.

With Snakes

1 Roll out a snake of clay from the same formula originally used to make the piece (see photo 29).

2 Brush water on the crack and wait a moment for it to soak into the clay.

3 Place the snake on top of the crack, and add a brush of water (see photo 30). Use the blender tool to push the material across the crack (see photo 31).

4 Use the side of the blender tool to wipe away any excess.

To mend a break, it's best to work directly on a kiln shelf. Run a line or coil of syringe on one side of the break and attach the other side using slip like glue. If the piece is flat, you can syringe one side of the break, then place the piece flat on the kiln shelf. Attach the other piece by sliding it in place and holding both sides together to the count of 10. When the syringe is dry, place the shelf directly in the kiln to be fired again. This way you don't have to move the piece and risk breaking the repair. After firing, remove the extra metal at the break using a jeweler's needle file.

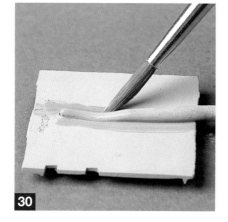

Firing Metal Clay

You can fire metal clay with a torch, hot pot, trinket kiln, speed fire cone, or metal clay kiln. There are two exceptions: First Generation clay needs to be fired in a kiln for two hours, and only Next Generation can be fired with the hot pot. I recommend using a kiln for firing most metal clay pieces, and for firing with glass, and natural and synthetic gemstones.

Torch Firing

Torch firing can be used for small pieces made of Second or Next Generation clay, and since a torch doesn't have a temperature gauge, it's possible to overheat and melt the piece. I learned to watch the fine silver change color as it goes through five specific firing stages. If you pay attention to the color changes you will be able to time the firing and recognize when the piece is fully sintered. It's a good idea to practice torch firing before using an actual piece.

Learning How to Torch Fire Metal Clay
To practice, my friend and colleague, Tim McCreight, suggests sacrificing a smidge of metal clay to the torch gods. Take a pea-size ball of metal clay, flatten it, and allow it to dry to bone dry. Place the piece on a solder pad and heat it to observe the stages and changes in the clay.

Watch as the binder burns away and the piece shrinks. Use the bushy part of the flame and heat the piece until it goes through these color changes: light pink, bright pink, dull red, and bright red glowing hot. Then, continue to heat the piece until it melts.

After the glowing hot stage, the piece will start to melt around the edges and begin to look like mercury. Keep heating and the piece of metal clay will puddle. Sintering happens between the bright pink and dull red color changes. You never want to heat your pieces to the bright glowing red stage. Once you have watched and learned to recognize these different color characteristics, you will have the confidence to torch fire without melting your work.

The Stages of Torch Firing
At stage one, the binder burns away and the piece begins to shrink (see photo 32).

Use the bushy part of the flame and heat the piece until it starts to glow light pink, this is stage two (see photo 33).

At stage three, the silver glows a bright pink to dull red; begin timing at this point (see photo 34).

Move the torch away if the color changes from dull red to a brilliant red-orange; this is stage four. At stage four, you're dangerously close to melting the piece, and if the edges of the piece glow a brilliant red-orange, and the surface is almost reflective, you're close to meltdown (see photo 35).

Stage five is meltdown (see photo 36).

Timing
Sintering happens at stage three, between the bright pink and dull red color changes. For Second Generation clay, start timing at stage three, and hold at this color for five minutes. For Next Generation clay, start timing at stage three, and hold the pink color for one minute.

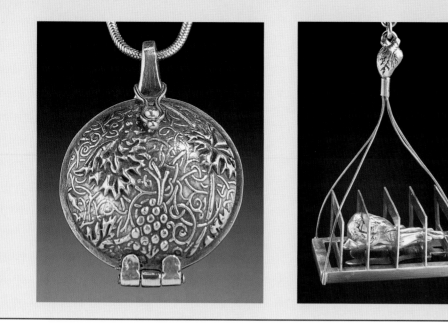

far left: **Susan J. Lewis**
Grape Locket, 2006
7.8 x 3.3 x 1.8 cm
Silver metal clay, sterling silver, silver black
patina, grape leaves; hollow constructed,
carved, hinged, slip-painted
Photo by Jerry L. Anthony

left: **Lorena Lazard**
Life Hangs by a Thread, 2005
8 x 4.3 x 3 cm
Sterling silver, silver metal clay, 14-karat gold
metal clay
Photo by Paolo Gori

Hot Pot, Trinket Kiln, and Speed Cone Firing

The hot pot, trinket kiln, and speed cone systems have advantages in portability and low price. If you're unsure about your commitment to metal clay, one of these kilns may be an excellent purchase until you're ready for a kiln. You are limited in the size and how many pieces you can fire at once with these systems. For the beginner, this is not a huge disadvantage. Follow manufacturer's directions for using the hot pot, trinket kiln, or speed cone firing systems.

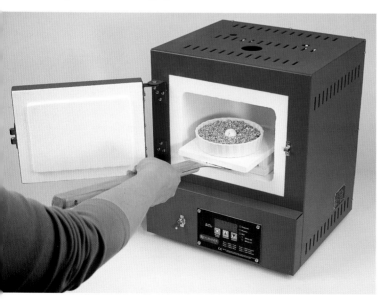

Kiln Firing

There are special kilns designed to fire metal clay that can also be used for small scale glass slumping, glass annealing, and traditional enameling. These small electric kilns are equipped with a programmable pyrometer (a device that allows you to reliably set the temperature and firing time) and don't need any special wiring since they plug into a regular three-prong outlet. To kiln fire, follow one of the firing schedules listed in the Metal Clay Formulas section, or follow the suggested firing schedule specific for each project. Kilns are available through the metal clay suppliers, and instructions on programming the kiln are included.

Kiln Safety

When setting up your workspace, you need to choose a safe place to fire the kiln. Kilns designed for firing metal clay are efficient and well insulated. However the back, sides, and top will get very hot, and you need to take this into consideration when choosing a place for your kiln. The bottom of a metal clay kiln is very well insulated, so it's safe to place them on most surfaces. I've fired my kiln on a kitchen counter, wooden table, and washing machine with no problems. The back and sides need to be at least one foot away from a wall or another object because they radiate so much heat.

Be certain that nothing is over the top of your kiln, such as a wooden bookshelf, etc. The top of the kiln

right: Terry Kovalcik
Dore Dore, 2005
5 x 1 x 0.8 cm
Silver metal clay, silver metal clay
paste; carved, molded, dried, filled,
sanded, and painted
Photo by Corrin Jacobsen Kovalcik

far right: Shahasp Valentine
Twig #3, Rosary Necklace, 2005
Pendant: 6 x 0.5 x 4 cm
Fine silver metal clay, pearls
Photo by artist

gets very hot—hot enough to burn your hand if you touch it during the firing process. Also, you need to consider the workspace around your kiln. I have a layer of brick on my counter to the right side of my kiln. Because I am right-handed and the kiln door opens to the left, this provided a safe area for loading and unloading hot kiln shelves.

Firing Safety

For all firing methods, it's a good idea to have a fire extinguisher at the ready. I've never needed it, but it's a smart safety choice to keep a fire extinguisher rated for electrical equipment close by, in plain view, and easily accessible.

Safety Tip

When you are firing anything organic in the clay, be certain to vent your kiln or fire outdoors. Organic material will combust at around 200°F (93°C) to 500°F (260°C) and can produce a great deal of smoke. Never open your kiln at this stage. The oxygen you introduce to the burning organic material can cause a flare-up and possibly burn you.

Surface Finish

When silver clay has been fired, it looks matte white (see photo 37). It doesn't appear silver at all. Gold comes out a matte ochre color. The surface of unpolished metal is uneven and porous. If we viewed a cross section under a microscope it would look like the cross section of a sponge. To achieve a shiny metal finish you need to abrade or burnish the surface. You can also do a combination of surface finishes on one piece. I have included my choice for surface finish for the projects covered in this book, but the choice is really up to you.

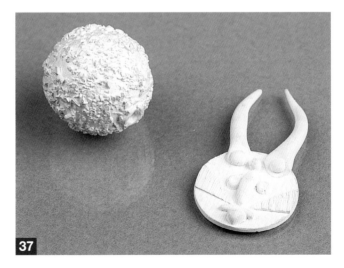

37

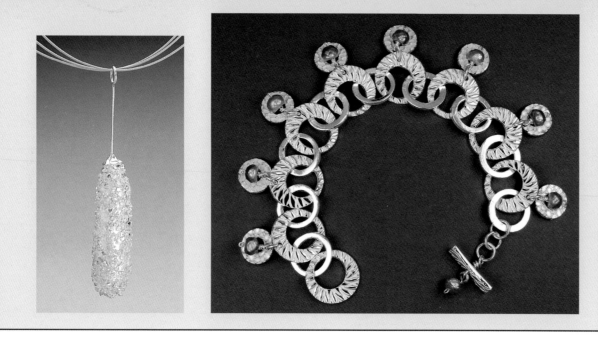

far left: Ann Davis
Arcyria Denudata, 2006
1.6 x 6.4 x 10.2 cm
Silver metal clay, fine silver, silver metal clay sheet; slip-painted, rolled in chunks, soldered
Photo by Jeff O'Dell

left: Maria Martinez
Morning Mist, 2006
22.9 x 1 x 0.3 cm
Silver metal clay, sterling silver; hand fabricated
Photo by David Castellanos

Abraded Finish

An abraded finish is achieved by sanding, filing, or grinding. In this type of finish, the high areas are removed, and when the surface is level the piece has an even shine. When sanding, filing, or grinding, what else will be removed? The surface texture. Because texture is one of the greatest creative assets available with metal clay, an abraded finish is usually not a good choice. However, a true mirror finish is an abraded finish, and it's simply stunning.

A mirror finish can be accomplished with a little elbow grease using a series of sandpapers with increasing grit number and decreasing abrasive size. An excellent use of a mirror finish is on the edges of a band ring. The sparkling finish will catch the light and draw attention to the piece. Also, it provides a smooth edge that is comfortable to slip on and off the finger. To get a mirror finish, start with a 400-grit sandpaper and work your way up to one of the ultra-fine grits of 1200 or more.

Making an abraded finish with a rotary tool

Burnishing

A burnished surface is achieved by pushing the high points so they are almost even with the low points. Think of mountains and valleys. In a burnished surface, you need to push the mountains down to the valleys, and the metal surface will shine.

A metal brush with liquid soap and water will give a satin finish. A soft satin finish can be produced by using a soft wire brush with liquid soap and water. Each wire in the metal brush acts as a burnisher.

Never dry brush your metal clay pieces. The porous surface will catch the metal wire and deposit a thin layer of that metal on the surface. A dry brass brush leaves a thin layer of brass, giving the silver a yellow cast, and a steel

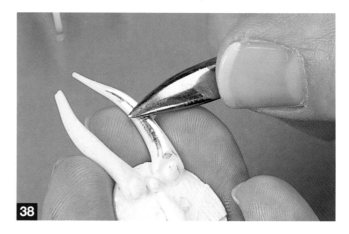
38

Pamela Morris Thomford
My Father, My Children, My Worry... A Mother's Prayer, 1999
101.6 x 6.4 x 1.3 cm
Sterling silver, silver metal clay, rubies, mica, photographs, rifle casings, patina; fabricated, cast, acid etched, riveted
Photos by Tim Thayer

brush will give an almost pewter finish. Always use soap and water for a wire brush finish.

To get a high polish in specific spots, a hand burnisher is rubbed across the surface of the fired piece (see photo 38). Hand burnishing can look almost as good as a mirror finish. A great place to hand burnish is around a stone. This highly reflective surface will draw attention to the stone and, by a trick of the eye, make the stone appear larger. Try burnishing the edges of earrings, as well. As they dangle, the light will catch the burnished edge and they'll twinkle.

Rotary tumbler with stainless steel shot

A high polish is best achieved with a rotary tumbler filled with stainless steel shot and a diluted burnishing solution. By placing your piece in the tumbler, the rolling action of the steel shot will push down the high areas. You'll shorten the time in the tumbler if you first wire brush your piece with soap and water. The longest I leave my metal clay piece in the tumbler is 45 minutes. Laboratory-grown stones, glass, and enameled pieces can safely go in the tumbler.

Patina

For pieces with an interesting texture, I apply the patina, then rub the surface with a polishing cloth. The color stays in the low area, and the high areas are polished to reveal the pure metal. In this way, patina is used to enhance the texture, not hide it.

There are many possibilities for using chemical patinas to obtain a wide range of colors. One of the most versatile and easily obtained patina solutions is liver of sulfur, also known as sulfurated potash. It can be used to achieve a rainbow of colors on silver. Liver of sulfur comes in either liquid or lump form and can be found through jeweler's supply and bead shops.

Liver of Sulfur Solution

I get the best results with the lump form of liver of sulfur. It can be mixed as needed, giving the user complete control over the concentration.

1 Place pea-size lump of solid liver of sulfur in a glass or plastic bowl, and add one cup (240 ml) of the hottest water you can get from the tap.

2 Allow the lump to dissolve. It will smell like rotten eggs and the water will turn a bright yellow-green color.

3 Fill another glass or plastic bowl with cold water. This will be your rinse water.

4 Be certain the metal clay piece is clean and free of grease or oil. Even the oil from your hands can resist the patina (see photo 39). Grip the metal clay piece with stainless steel tweezers, dip the piece in the liver-of-sulfur solution and swish it around for about two seconds.

39

5 Dip the piece in the rinse water (see photo 40). Reposition the tweezers and repeat the process until you get the color you like (see photos 41 and 42). When you are happy with the results, hold the piece under cold running water for one minute. If the piece is hollow, such as a bead, it may be necessary to soak the piece in fresh water to remove the solution from inside the form.

6 The final rinse is a solution of one cup (240 ml) fresh water with one tablespoon (15 ml) of baking soda to stop the acid from continuing to color the piece.

Liver of Sulfur Patina Color Progression

- One dip: Silver metal clay turns to a golden yellow. It almost looks like gold.

- Two dips: The gold color changes to rose.

- Three dips: The rose color becomes darker and changes to a glowing magenta.

- Four dips: The patina will be red-violet.

- Five dips: The color changes to blue-purple.

- Six dips: The surface will be steel blue, from here the patina begins to lose its color and starts turning gray and then black.

- Seven dips: The patina will be blue-gray.

- Eight dips: The piece is blue-black, a color I find interesting because of its richness and depth.

- Additional dips: The patina will become jet-black.

40

41

42

Barbara Becker Simon
Red Rockets, 2005
50.8 x 2.5 x 5.1 cm
Silver metal clay, assorted rocks, stainless steel
Photo by Larry Sanders

If you'd like a black patina, go through all the color changes (see photo 43) to develop the patina slowly. If you just plunk the piece in the liver-of-sulfur solution and let it sit at the bottom of the solution without rinsing between color changes, the black can build up too quickly and can flake off. If you don't like the patina, it can easily be removed with a dip and rinse in silver tarnish remover, silver polish, or a polishing cloth.

Safety Note

Liver of sulfur is a mild chemical, but you should be careful when using it. Use tweezers to dip your piece in the solution. The containers you use need to be glass or plastic. Do not use the containers again for any other use after they have come in contact with this chemical solution. In my studio, I use empty plastic containers, one to mix the liver of sulfur, one for the rinse water, and one for the final rinse with baking soda. The solution will be inert after 24 hours and can be flushed down the toilet for disposal. When I finish a project, the plastic containers get a good rinse and go to the curb with the recycling.

43

Stones

Stones can be either natural or man-made. Natural stones are the real deal, no faking. A man-made gemstone is created to look like or imitate the real thing. In gemology, the term synthetic describes a gemstone that has the same chemical composition and crystal structure as the natural counterpart. The terms lab-created and lab-grown mean the same as synthetic. A simulant is any material intended to resemble a natural stone. Glass, plastic, or a combination of layered glass on top of a paper backing are all materials used to simulate the look of a natural stone.

To understand the difference, let's consider two different types of man-made rubies. A synthetic ruby is a laboratory-grown stone made to look like a natural ruby. A simulated ruby could be a piece of red glass cut to look like a natural ruby. These terms are important to understand when purchasing stones to use in combination with firing metal clay. If you fire a simulated stone made of glass it will melt or burn up in the kiln. Generally, we will be using synthetic stones as an inclusion with metal clay.

Fire-in-place stones open a world of creative possibilities.

Pre-Firing Inclusions

Natural and man-made gemstones, glass, and porcelain can be fired with your metal clay pieces. In fact, anything fired with metal clay is called an inclusion.

Beyond Metal Clay: Gemstones, Glass, and Porcelain

Metal clay by itself has amazing potential. However, combining it with other materials gives you the opportunity for rich and diverse artistic exploration. The materials often play off each other in a mutually beneficial way. For example, a ring of gold is beautiful, but a gold ring set with a row of cubic zirconias is stunning, just like the Gold and Cubic Zirconia Ring on page 122.

Natural Gemstones for Kiln Firing

Because Mother Nature controls the formation of natural gemstones, there is no way to guarantee that a natural stone will survive kiln or torch firing. Inclusion material, trapped air, or some other impurity could have a negative effect on the outcome. However, the stones on this list survived testing and are recommended to fire in Next Generation metal clay in a fast-ramping kiln (a kiln that will climb to a high temperature quickly) at 1110°F (600°C) for 45 minutes.

Chrome Diopside
Almandine Garnet
Pyrope Garnet
Rhodolite Garnet
Tsavorite Garnet
Hematite
Moonstone
Peridot
Black Star Sapphire

In a slow-ramping kiln test, the kiln was ramped 500°F (260°C) per hour to a firing temperature of 1110°F (600°C), and held at 1110°F (600°C) for 45 minutes. This list of natural stones fired in Next Generation metal clay are recommended as a good bet.

Tanzanite
Green Topaz
White Topaz
Green Tourmaline

Natural Gemstones for Torch Firing

These natural gemstones are recommended to fire in Next Generation metal clay with a butane torch at 1110°F (600°C) for 3 minutes.

Rhodolite
Peridot
Blue Sapphire (A-Grade)
Blue Sapphire (AAA-Grade)
White Sapphire
Ruby (A-Grade)
Ruby (AAA-Grade)
Tanzanite

Synthetic Gemstones for Kiln Firing

The synthetic stones on this list survived the testing and are recommended to fire in Next Generation metal clay in a fast-ramping kiln at 1110°F (600°C) for 45 minutes.

Alexandrite
Cubic Zirconia
Emerald
Ruby
Sapphire
Spinel

Synthetic Gemstones for Torch Firing

These synthetic gemstones are recommended to fire in Next Generation metal clay with a butane torch at 1110°F (600°C) for 3 minutes.

Blue Spinel
White Sapphire
White Cubic Zirconia
Green Garnet

Stone Setting

My background in traditional metalsmithing has trained me in a variety of different stone setting techniques. Fire-in-place stone setting is the simplest setting method I have ever used. By taking advantage of the shrinkage in all formulas of metal clay, you can set stones and other inclusions. Friction is what holds the stone in place and is often referred to by jewelers as "friction set," or "friction setting."

Ball Setting

A ball setting is best used for round stones.

1 Roll a tiny ball of metal clay at least the same diameter as the stone (see photo 44).

2 Choose where you would like to have the stone setting, and brush the area with a light amount of water.

3 Set the ball in place and flatten the ball slightly with a clear plastic lid (see photo 45). This allows you to watch the clay as you flatten the ball.

4 Cut a hole in the center of the flattened ball (see photo 46).

5 Press a conical tip blender tool in the hole (see photo 47).

6 Using the craft knife with a bit of olive oil balm on the tip, lift the stone and place it in the hole (see photo 48).

7 Use the end of a coffee stirrer to press the stone down below the surface (1/16 inch [1.6 mm] if using Second or Next Generation clay, and 1/8 inch [3 mm] for First Generation) (see photos 49 and 50).

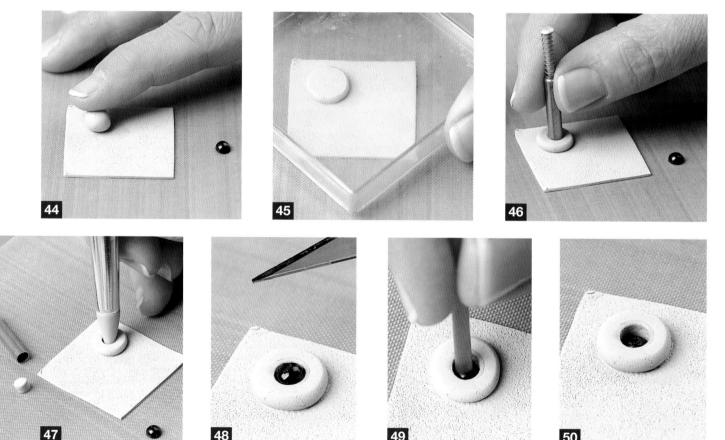

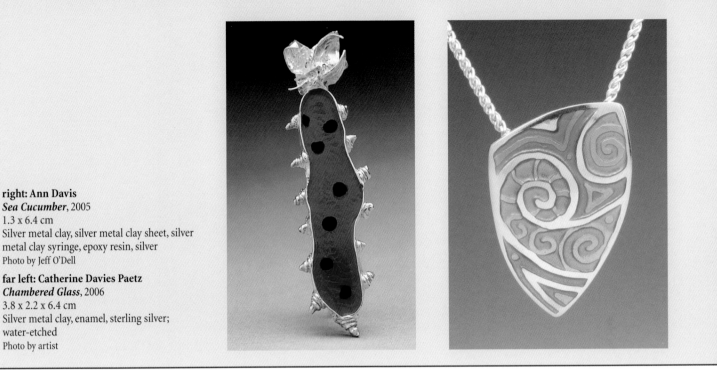

right: **Ann Davis**
Sea Cucumber, 2005
1.3 x 6.4 cm
Silver metal clay, silver metal clay sheet, silver metal clay syringe, epoxy resin, silver
Photo by Jeff O'Dell

far left: **Catherine Davies Paetz**
Chambered Glass, 2006
3.8 x 2.2 x 6.4 cm
Silver metal clay, enamel, sterling silver; water-etched
Photo by artist

Syringe Setting

Any shaped stone can be held in place with metal clay syringe.

1 Cut a hole in the metal clay where you would like to set the stone.

2 Use the metal clay syringe to create a coil of metal clay around the opening (see photo 51).

3 Set the stone over the opening and press the stone down ¹/₁₆ inch (1.6 mm) below the surface of the syringe coil (see photos 52 and 53). The stone will be held in place when the material shrinks.

Zahava Lambert
Thistle Necklace, 2006
19 x 19 cm
Silver metal clay syringe, thistle
leaves, moonstone bezels, silver
wire; syringed
Photo by artist

Carved Setting and Bur Setting

You can use this technique to set oval, fire-in-place stones. This technique can be adapted for square, rectangle, and triangle-shaped stones.

1 Start by balling up a pea-size piece of moist clay. Flatten the pea between your fingers to ¼ inch (6 mm) thick.

2 Use an oval clay cutter and cut out an oval shape that will be larger than the stone by ¼ inch (6 mm).

3 Punch out the center of the oval piece with a drinking straw.

4 Allow it to dry to bone dry, then use a pencil to trace the shape of the stone (see photo 54).

5 Carve a small amount of material at a time, using the stone to check your fit (see photos 55 and 56). When you achieve a tight fit, you're done.

6 Use a brush of water to hold the stone setting in place.

54

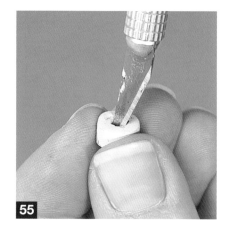

55

56

Bur Setting

For a circular stone, you can use the bur setting. Instead of carving a place to hold the stone (as in the carved setting), the inside can be cut with a stone cutting bur using a motorized flexible shaft.

1 Start by balling up a pea-sized piece of clay. Flatten the pea between your fingers to ¼ inch (6 mm) thick.

2 Use a brass plunger cutter or drinking straw to cut a plug that will be larger than the stone diameter by ¼ inch (6 mm). Allow the plug to dry to bone dry.

3 Use a sliding gauge or calipers to determine the stone size in millimeters (see photo 57). Use the same tool to find the corresponding size cutting bur (see photo 58).

4 Use a craft knife to drill out a depression in the center of the plug

5 Use the bur in the flex shaft to take away the right amount of material to hold the stone (see photos 59 and 60).

6 With a bit of olive oil balm on the tip of a craft knife lift the stone and place in the hole (see photo 61).

7 A brush of water will hold the stone in place.

57

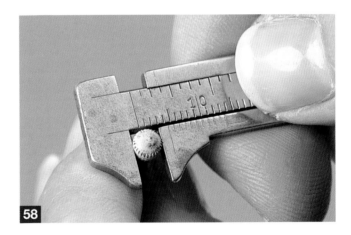
58

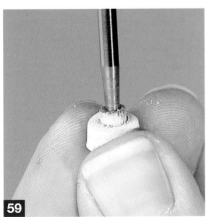
59

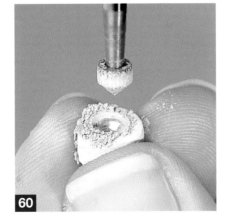
60

61

Layered Slab Setting

Facet cut stones of any shape can be set this way.

1. Roll out Second or Next Generation metal clay to the thickness of three playing cards.

2. Use a brass cutter to cut a shape that will be the top layer to hold the stone (see photo 62).

3. Use a circular cutter to cut a hole in the shaped piece from step 2 that is only 1/16 inch (1.6 mm) larger than the stone (see photo 63).

4. To make the backing piece, cut out another shape of clay larger than the first.

5. Cut a small opening (1/8 inch [3 mm] smaller than the diameter of the stone) in the backing layer to create a shelf on which the stone will sit. Having a small hole behind the stone will allow light to shine through and illuminate the stone.

6. With a damp brush, moisten the top of the backing layer and the underside of the top piece.

7. Press the backing piece and shaped piece together lightly, and wet the edges to assure a good seam. Place the stone in the circular opening.

62

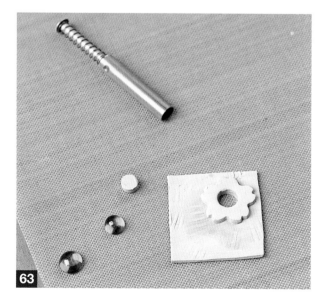

63

Slip Dip Setting

This setting works on cabochon cut stones of any size.

1 Glue the domed side of a fire-in-place cabochon stone to a bamboo skewer with fabric glue.

2 Dip the flat end of the stone into a jar of commercially prepared slip (see photo 64).

3 Cover the stone two-thirds up the side, twisting as you lift out of the jar (see photo 65).

4 Poke the bamboo skewer into a piece of foam and let the slip dry.

5 Repeat steps 2 and 3, to build up three layers of slip, allowing them to dry between each layer.

6 Peel the stone from the glue, and then sand the back flat with a fine emery board.

7 Glue the setting in place on your piece with syringed slip.

64

65

Nicole Michelle Beatrice
Untitled, 2005
4 x 6 x 0.2 cm
Silver metal clay, blue zircon stones,
liver of sulfur patina
Photo by artist

Paper Setting

In this technique, a small square of paper clay is used to hold an inverted stone in place. These directions work to hold a 4-mm fire-in-place stone, but you can alter the measurements to hold larger stones. Facet-cut stones of any shape can be set this way.

1 Cut a ¼-inch (6 mm) square of sheet metal clay.

66

67

2 Using a craft knife, cut an X in the center of the square, but don't cut too close to the edge (see photo 66). Stop about ¹⁄₁₆ inch (1.6 mm) from the corners.

3 Roll out a slab of Second Generation clay to the thickness of three playing cards.

4 Dry the slab to bone dry, then cut a hole with the craft knife precisely where you would like to set the stone. Be careful not to cut the hole larger than the stone, or it could fall out from the back of the piece.

5 Place the stone inverted (upside down) and centered on top of the hole. Lightly brush water around the stone (see photo 67).

6 Lay the square piece with the X cut on top of the stone. The stone will peek through the X cut (see photo 68).

7 Carefully brush water around the outside edge of the square piece of the sheet clay holding the stone.

68

Glass

Glass is an unpredictable material to use with metal clay. You'll want to experiment and keep detailed notes about everything you try. Changing one variable may dramatically alter your results. Remember, failures are as good as successes when you're exploring new ideas.

Dichroic Glass

Dichroic glass has been used with metal clay for years and it's no longer considered experimental. Here's how to bezel-set a dichroic glass cabochon:

1 Make the bezel to hold the dichroic glass cabochon in place. Roll out a snake of metal clay. The diameter of the snake needs to be one-half to three-quarters the height of the cabochon, and long enough to wrap loosely around the glass cabochon (see photo 69).

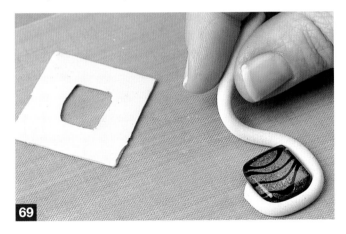
69

2 Next, wrap the snake around the dichroic glass cabochon, overlap the seam, and cut away the extra. Lightly press the coil down around the stone. Be certain the seam on the bottom and the overlapping seam are well attached. Brush water on both seams. This is important to ensure the glass will not seep out the bottom of the bezel during the firing. Dry the piece thoroughly.

3 Fire the piece at 1470°F (800°C) for 25 to 30 minutes. When the firing is complete, open the door to rapidly cool the piece until the pyrometer reads 1000°F (538°C). Then quickly shut the kiln door. This is called

crash cooling, and it prevents devitrification, or clouding, of the glass. Allow the piece to cool to room temperature before opening the kiln door again. Even though you might be tempted, don't peek! If the glass cools too quickly it could crack.

Clear Window Glass

Windowpane glass is also known as float glass, and its chemical makeup can vary greatly. Some turn a noticeable green cast after firing, and some turn amber. Often, when you fire the same piece multiple times, the glass becomes more opaque.

Colored Sheet Glass

When working with colored glass, you need to know what the Coefficient of Expansion (known as COE) is for the brand of glass you are using. The COE is the measurable difference between the glass when it is hot and when it is cool. Hot glass expands and then contracts as it cools. When combining glass colors, you need to use compatible glass, or when the piece is annealing and cooling, the different expansion and cooling rates will crack the glass. Always remember to use the same COE, and you should be fine. For our needs, it is best to stick to one color. Knowing the COE will determine the firing time and temperature. For example, glass with a COE of 96 fires at 1350°F (732°C) for 30 minutes.

Porcelain

Since it's fired at much higher temperatures than metal clay, porcelain makes a terrific inclusion material. However, keep in mind that metal clay will shrink, but the porcelain will not. Take advantage of the lower shrinkage rate of either Second or Next Generation metal clay (between 10 and 15 percent) when designing pieces to be fired with porcelain.

Post-Firing Inclusions

These surface design techniques can bring another layer of sophistication to your work. Epoxy, resin inlay, kum boo, and enameling benefit greatly from good planning and design work and shouldn't be an afterthought. I view these techniques as surface design, and the colors, shapes and patterns need to relate to the whole piece for a visually successful result. That's not to say I haven't improved the aesthetics of a piece long after the design process with the addition of kum boo gold foil. However, this is the exception rather than the rule.

Epoxy Inlay

A two-part epoxy can be used as an inlay material. Be sure to use a non-yellowing formula of industrial strength two-part epoxy. You can find this in jewelry supply stores or online.

Mix the epoxy according to manufacturer's instructions. Add powdered pigment, ground spices, or acrylic paint to get the color or effect you want (see photos 70 and 71). Use a plastic spoon to load the colored epoxy into the piece (see photo 72). Push it into large areas with a craft stick or small areas with a toothpick. The epoxy will set in five minutes, but may take at least 24 hours for the epoxy to cure. If the epoxy layer is thick, it may take a few days to cure.

Finish by sanding the piece, facedown, in a shallow dish with water, using 1000-grit wet/dry sandpaper. Why sand under water? Breathing the dust from this material carries a significant health risk. Holding a piece underwater as you sand it will eliminate this risk.

Andrea Wagner
Inside-Out Box Brooches, 2005
4 to 6 x 2.5 to 4 x 1.75 to 2.3 cm
Pure silver, sterling silver; silver metal
clay applied to cardboard, fired and
hand fabricated
Photo by artist

Kum Boo

Kum boo is an ancient Korean metalworking technique combining fine silver and gold. It has enjoyed a modern rebirth due to the increased popularity of jewelry pieces that combine silver and gold. It's a relatively inexpensive technique for adding a bit of gold to fine silver.

You'll need 24-karat gold foil, a heat source, long tweezers, heat-resistant gloves, a burnishing tool, a bamboo

skewer, trivet kiln with a brass plate insert, and a metal clay piece directly from the kiln. Using tweezers, take the metal clay piece from the kiln and set it on the brass plate designed to use with the trivet kiln. Cut the 24-karat gold to the design you want for your piece. Be sure not to touch the gold with your bare hands. Oils and dirt from your fingers will inhibit the two metals from forming a bond. Place the foil between tracing paper to cut it, or cut it between the tissue paper it comes wrapped in (see photo 73).

To test if your piece is hot enough for the silver and gold to bond, set the blunt end of a bamboo skewer on the metal clay piece. When it starts to smoke and turn black (see photo 74), the piece is at the correct temperature for bonding. Place the gold on top of the silver and tack it down with the burnishing tool (see photo 75). Burnish the piece across the gold foil, and it will permanently attach to the fine silver. This technique will only work on unpolished silver.

far left: **Robert Dancik**
Tri-checked Reflector, 2006
5 x 3.8 x 1.2 cm
Silver metal clay, concrete,
sterling silver, synthetic ruby,
epoxy resin
Photo by Douglas Foulke

left: **Pamela Morris Thomford**
Sneaky Pete, 2001
8.2 x 3.2 x 2.6 cm
Sterling silver, silver metal clay,
fine silver; fabricated, roller
printed, cast
Photo by Keith Meiser

Enameling

Enameling is a diverse technique. For the projects in this book, we will touch on a very introductory use of enamel.

True jewelry enamel is referred to as vitreous enamel. Essentially, it's powdered glass ground to a fine mesh, similar to the consistency of sand. Vitreous enamel is very compatible with fine silver and high-karat gold (which is exactly what metal clay is). This powdered glass can be applied to a fired and polished piece of metal clay in many ways. In this book, we'll be sifting it on in dry form and packing it into place as a wet mixture (also called wet-packed).

Dry Application

When applying enamel in a dry state, it's sifted through a small screen onto the surface of the fired and polished metal clay (see photo 76). More enamel should be sifted onto the edges than in the center of the piece. The edges of the metal heat first during firing, and the enamel will

76

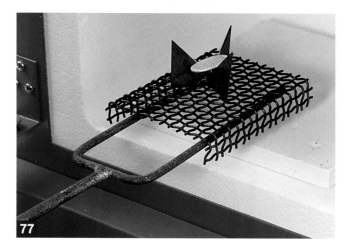

77

right: **Terry Kovalcik**
Fiddleheads, 2006
6 x 2 x 1.2 cm
Silver metal clay, silver metal clay sheet, silver metal clay paste, sterling silver beads and chain, oxidized liver of sulfur
Photo by Corrin Jacobsen Kovalcik

far right: **Shahasp Valentine**
Twig #1, Choker, 2005
6.6 x 0.7 x 4 cm
Fine silver metal clay, pearls
Photo by artist

burn away on the edges faster than in the center. The idea is to have more enamel on the edges, so by the time the center has fused, there will still be a nice layer of enamel remaining on the edges. Place in a hot kiln at 1500°F (815°C) until the glass powder melts and fuses to the silver (see photo 77).

If there isn't enough enamel on the edges, the uneven surface tension will result in a cracked piece. There is a way to fix this: grind down the piece with an alundum stone (a sanding stone) under water, apply more enamel, and fire the piece again. Of course, the goal is to not let this happen. An even layer of fused enamel will last forever, or close to it.

Wet Packing

For the wet packing technique, enamel is mixed with distilled water and a binding agent. The enamel can be mixed with a lot of water and binder and applied much like watercolor, using a watercolor brush to paint the surface in a loose and flowing way. By using less water and binder, the enamel could resemble oil paint. For this effect, a plastic palette knife is used to trough on the enamel. Wet packing is traditionally used in the champlevè technique. Champlevè is inlaid enamel.

To wet pack a recessed area, start with a teaspoon amount of powdered enamel mixed with a few drops of distilled water and one drop of binding agent. This mixture is packed into low recessed areas of the design by lifting a small amount of the enamel mixture with a plastic spoon, then shoveling it into the low areas with a pusher (dental tool or fine quality watercolor brush). The wet enamel is packed into the recessed area, giving it an inlaid appearance.

It's very important to fire the enamel only after it's completely dry. Wet enamel still has water in it. When placed in a hot kiln, the water will boil and splatter enamel all over the inside of your kiln. Try speed drying your wet-packed piece on the top of the kiln to dry it thoroughly before firing. Fire in a hot kiln at 1500°F (815°C) until the enamel melts and the surface is glassy and reflective.

CHAPTER 4

Projects

The 25 projects in this book were chosen so you'll learn various techniques by actually doing them. The projects range in complexity from very basic to moderately difficult. In the end, your knowledge and appreciation for the medium of metal clay will be greater, and you'll have beautiful results and stunning jewelry to show for it.

Metal Clay Project Tool Kits

You'll quickly notice that there are specific tools used repeatedly on practically every metal clay project. In order to abbreviate the length of the supply lists in the following projects, I suggest you make a personal tool kit to carry with you from project to project. For clarity, we'll call the Metal Clay Tool Kit for the rest of this book, and it will appear at the top of each project's tool and material list. With this list of tools in hand, you'll be ready for anything.

Plastic rolling pin
Playing cards
Mat board spacers
Blender tool
Needle tool
Craft knife
Flexible tissue blade
Emery boards, fine and coarse
Tweezers
Brass brush
Watercolor brush
Wet wipes
Olive oil hand balm
Permanent marker
Pencil
Rigid and flexible work surfaces
A dish of water

Embossed Bolo

Slab construction is a wonderful way to work with metal clay. Adding embossed textures to the clay with homemade stamps carved from art erasers lets you create truly one-of-a-kind designs.

Embossed Bolo

Tools & Materials

Metal clay tool kit,
   (see page 66)

White plastic eraser

Carving tool with No. 1 and
   No. 2 V tips

Blender tools with No. 0 and
   No. 6 tips

Olive oil hand balm

Flexible worksheet

Next Generation metal clay,
   26 grams

Syringe metal clay

Plastic texture sheet

Brass plunger cutter, sizes
   ⅜, ⁷⁄₁₆, and ⅝ inch (9.5 mm,
   1.1 cm, and 1.6 cm)

Drinking straw, ³⁄₁₆-inch
   (5 mm) diameter

Terra-cotta saucer filled with
   vermiculite

Liver of sulfur

Polishing cloth

Two-part epoxy

Leather bolo cord, 42 inches
   (106.6 cm), 4 mm

Instructions

1 Use a pencil to draw a pattern on one side of the white plastic eraser, and a different pattern on the other side. Experiment with crosshatching, weave patterns, or simple lines, but keep it simple. Carve the patterns with the carving tool with the No. 1 or No. 2 V tips. Use the No. 6 blender tool to work the olive oil hand balm into the carved pattern on both sides of the eraser.

2 On the flexible worksheet, roll out a slab of Next Generation metal clay to the thickness of mat board. Set the carved eraser on top and press hard to get a deep impression of your first pattern. Trim the newly textured clay with a tissue blade to make two pieces measuring ½ x 2 inches (1.3 x 5 cm). Repeat the process using the second carved pattern on the eraser. Trim the newly textured clay to make two pieces measuring ⁷⁄₁₆ x 2 inches (1.1 x 5 cm). Let the pieces sit for 5 minutes before peeling them off the flexible worksheet. Place them texture-side-up on a hot plate to dry.

3 Use metal clay syringe to glue the four edges together to make a hollow box. Place a line of syringe down the edge of the ⁷⁄₁₆-inch-wide (1.1 cm) piece. Attach to the inside edge of the ½-inch (1.3 cm) piece, then hold the pieces together and count to 10. The pieces should sit for 5 minutes before transferring to the hot plate to finish drying. Repeat until all four walls are constructed. Sand the ends of the square shaped tubing with the coarse emery board.

4 To make the end pieces, roll out more Next Generation metal clay on top of a plastic texture sheet to the thickness of mat board. Cut two squares, ¾-inch (1.9 cm) each. Place them texture-side-down onto the hot plate. When they're dry, glue them in place with the syringe clay. Run a line of syringe on the end of the square tube and set the square in place. There will be a ¹⁄₁₆ inch (1.6 mm) ledge. Wipe away the extra syringe clay that squirts out with the smaller blender tool. Apply the extra material (on the blender tool) to the inside seam to reinforce the box construction from the inside. Nothing wasted! Repeat on the other end to close the box. Let the pieces dry.

5 To accommodate the leather cord, use the tip of the craft knife as a drill and cut a hole in the top and bottom of the box. Carve the hole a little larger than the diameter of the cord. Remember, this formula of clay will shrink between 10 and 15 percent.

6 To make the donut-shaped caps for the cord holes (see photo 1), roll out a marble-size ball of clay to the thickness of three playing cards, and cut two circles with the ⅝-inch (1.6 cm) cutter, then cut the centers with ⅜-inch (9.5 mm) cutter. Moisten with a brush of water around the holes, and attach the donut shapes to the ends (over the carved holes) by pressing lightly with your finger.

7 To make the tips for the ends of the leather cord (see photo 2), you'll need a drinking straw 3/16-inch (5 mm) in diameter. Cut off two pieces of the straw, each 2 inches (5 cm) long. Roll out Next Generation metal clay on a textured work surface to the thickness of three playing cards. Cut a 1 x 13/16-inch (2.5 x 2.1 cm) rectangle, and wrap it around one of the straw pieces. Next, use the No. 0 blender tool to close and blend the seam. Repeat this series of steps to make a second tip. Set both pieces on the hot plate to dry to bone dry.

8 Roll out a marble-size piece of metal clay to the thickness of mat board on a textured work surface. Cut out two circles with a 7/16-inch (1.1 cm) cutter. Place them onto the hot plate for 5 minutes. Take the straw pieces off the hot plate and slide the straw out of each piece of tubing. Sand the ends with the coarse emery board. Use metal clay syringe to glue a circle onto one end of each tube. There will be a 1/16-inch (1.6 mm) overhang.

9 Fire all three pieces (the box and two tips) in a terra-cotta saucer filled with vermiculite at 1650°F (900°C) for 2 hours. When cool, give the piece a satin finish by using a brass brush with soap and water. Dip the pieces in a liver-of-sulfur solution for a patina that will emphasize the texture. Rub with a polishing cloth, then assemble. To attach the bolo tips, mix a nickel-size amount of an industrial strength two-part epoxy and glue them onto the ends of the leather cord.

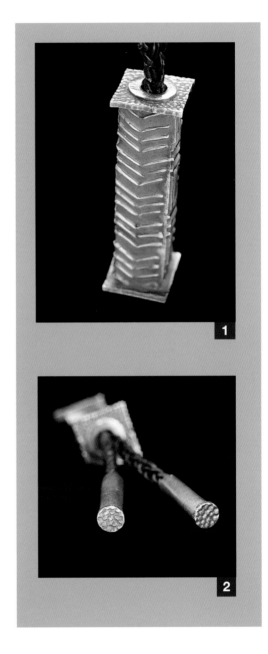

Bead Transformation

Covering porcelain bisque beads with metal clay slip lets you create uniformly shaped silver or gold beads quickly and easily. Add interesting textures to the forms by rolling the freshly painted forms in flakes of dried clay.

Metal clay tool kit,
(see page 66)

Porcelain bead blanks

Commercially prepared slip,
Second or Next Generation

Coffee stirrer

Linoleum tool

Terra-cotta saucer filled with
vermiculite

Wire brush

Silk cord

Instructions

1 Use the watercolor brush to cover each bisque-fired bead with a layer of commercially prepared slip directly from the jar. Make sure to paint down inside the holes. Pay close attention to the holes, because if you don't, they will crack due to surface tension from the metal clay shrinkage. Let each bead dry. Paint another layer of slip, then roll the wet pieces in chunks of what I call "dry stuff," to build up an interesting texture. This texturing material could be the discarded plugs from using the coffee stirrer like a cookie cutter, or the pieces you carve with a carving tool, or any of the dry bits left on your work surface at the end of the day. I keep this type of stuff in a small plastic container. You can repeat painting and layering texture as often as you like. I recommend at least four layers if you don't want the silver to burn away, develop cracks, or peel.

2 Fire the beads at 1650°F (900°C) for 10 minutes for Second Generation slip, or fire them at 1290°F (700°C) for 10 minutes for Next Generation slip. Support the beads in a terra-cotta plant saucer filled with vermiculite.

3 Finish each piece with a wire brush and soap and water. Use the burnisher to rub across the higher textures for a contrast between the two surfaces. This will create visual depth. String the beads on a paper clip and dip in liver of sulfur to get the color you like (see page 51). Rinse thoroughly and rub with a polishing cloth wrapped around an emery board. The hard backing will allow the cloth to wipe away the patina in the high areas. This method is better than using a cloth without a backing, because the soft cushion end of your fingertips would allow the patina to be wiped off in the low areas as well. This patina will emphasize the difference between the high and low areas of the texture.

4 When you achieve the surface you like, wash the beads with soap and water to remove the residue from polishing. String the pieces on a silk cord. Tie knots between the beads for a dramatic piece.

Simple Stud Earrings

Here's a great way to use metal clay remnants. Making stud earrings is quick, easy, a lot of fun, and good practice for mastering a new material.

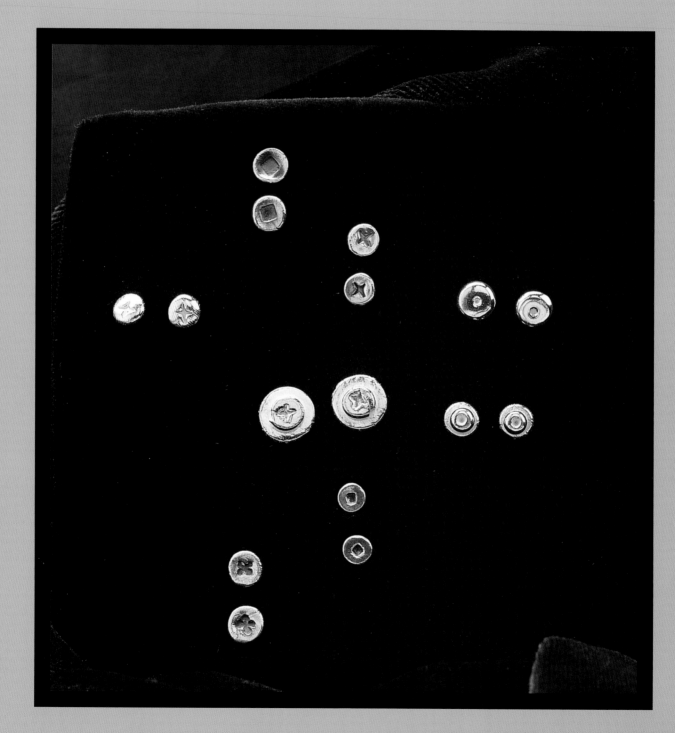

Tools & Materials

Metal clay tool kit,
    (see page 66)

Next Generation metal clay,
    5 grams

Clear plastic ruler

Texture makers: X-shaped
    coffee stirrer, ball point
    pen, marker, etc.

22-karat gold slip

Butane torch and fuel

Kiln shelf

Glass bowl filled with cold
    water

Hard silver solder

Sterling silver earring posts
    with 4 mm pads

Butane torch and fuel

Paste flux

Rotary tumbler with mixed
    stainless steel shot and
    liquid burnishing com-
    pound

Towel and Plastic strainer

Sterling silver friction ear nuts

Instructions

1 Roll a pea-size ball of Next Generation metal clay, and cut in half with the craft knife. Roll the two halves into balls, then press them flat with the clear plastic ruler. Brush the tops with a little water and set them aside while you make the next layer.

2 Start with just half the amount of clay used in step 1. Roll it into a small ball. Cut it in half. Ball up one half and set on top of one of the flattened disks. Using the clear plastic ruler, flatten the new top layer. Repeat for the other earring.

3 Press a texture into the center of the top layer. For the X pattern, I used a red coffee stirrer stick. Look for texture possibilities on the end of pens, golf tees, toothpicks, ends of screwdrivers, etc. There are lots of possible variations, so explore and have fun!

4 To make gold earrings, paint three coats of the 22-karat gold slip on the area of your choice. Remember, let the gold slip air dry thoroughly between applications. To make the all silver versions skip this step.

5 Be certain the textured clay discs are bone dry. Torch fire the disks on a kiln shelf with a butane torch. Lift the discs with tweezers and drop them in a bowl of cold water to quench. (Don't quench earrings this way that contain 22-karat gold slip. Air cool them.) Use the burnishing tool to hand-burnish the backs. Solder one sterling silver post to the back of each disc using the butane torch, hard silver solder, and paste flux.

6 Finish the earrings in a tumbler with stainless steel shot and burnishing compound. Because these are small earrings, it's best to empty the contents of the tumbler onto a towel placed inside a plastic strainer to find every piece. (Another option is to patina some pieces with liver of sulfur, then finish with a polishing cloth.) To complete, secure the earring backs to the earring studs.

Spiral Galaxy

In ancient societies, the spiral represented a journey: clockwise showed outward migration, while a counterclockwise motion signified a homecoming. Experiment with the process of adding gold slip to silver clay and see where it leads.

Tools & Materials

Metal clay tool kit,
(see page 66)

Plastic texture sheet

Next Generation metal clay,
6.5 grams

Hot plate

Sheet form of metal clay,
rectangle shape

22-karat gold slip

High quality synthetic bristle
watercolor brush for gold
slip, size No. 1

Spiral paper punch

Kiln shelf

Butane torch and fuel

Jeweler's soft brass brush

Small burnishing tool

Pair of gold vermeil headpins

12 semi precious stone
beads, (6) 5 mm, (6) 3 mm

Needle-nose pliers

Gold vermeil earwires

Instructions

1 Roll out the Next Generation metal clay on top of the plastic texture sheet to the thickness of three playing cards. Use the tissue blade to cut out two squares that measure ¾ inch (1.9 cm) each. Peel the squares away from the plastic texture sheet and set it texture side up on a hot plate to dry.

2 From the rectangular piece of sheet clay, cut a piece ¾ x 1¼ inches (1.9 x 3.2 cm) long. Coat the sheet clay with three thin layers of 22-karat gold slip. The consistency of the gold slip should be like nail polish. You can add water and mix with a pin tool to get this desired consistency. When the gold dries on the pin tool, it can be peeled off and added back to the gold slip container. The first layer of gold should be painted long ways, end to end with the synthetic bristle watercolor brush. Paint the gold to within ⅛ inch (3 mm) of the edges. Don't try to paint to the very edge, it's too tricky to control. Allow the gold layer to air dry, and paint the next layer the short way from side to side. Let the slip air dry and repeat the process. Allow the gold-covered sheet clay to air dry overnight.

3 Using the paper punch with a spiral design, punch one spiral with the gold side up and one with the silver side up. This will make matched spiral designs, perfect for earrings.

4 Place the squares back to back, and sand the edges with a fine emery board until they match. Place the pieces faceup on the work surface. Use the craft knife as a drill and cut holes in the top center of each square, ⅛ inch (3 mm) from the top edge.

5 With the squares faceup on the worktable, brush the surface of each with a generous amount of water. Position the spirals with the gold side up in the center of each square and press lightly with your finger. Check all the edges of each spiral for a good attachment. Press down any place that is not fully attached. You may need to add more water.

6 Set the squares on the hot plate to dry. Touch up any gold areas as needed. Set back on the hot plate to dry thoroughly. Set the earrings on a kiln shelf and torch fire with a butane torch (see page 45 for more on this technique). Fire for 1 minute once you see the gold glowing a vibrant pink hue.

7 Finish the pieces with a soft brass brush, then hand-burnish the gold with a small burnishing tool. String semiprecious stone beads onto a pair of gold vermeil head pins. Use needlenose pliers to make a simple loop at the top of each wire, twisting the wire to secure the loops. Add the gold vermeil ear wires to complete.

Domino Theory

As I began working on these earrings, I realized the potential for a high contrast design. Since I love the bold design of dominoes, one thing naturally led to another.

Metal clay tool kit,
(see page 66)

Cork-backed ruler

White sheet glass,
⅛ inch (3 mm)

Oil-fed glass cutter, or glass
cutter and glass cutting oil

Glass breaking pliers

Alundum stone

Rectangle shape (3 x 12 cm)
sheet metal clay

Rigid work surface

Watercolor brush, size No. 1

Commercially prepared slip

Hot plate

Paper punch, ¼-inch (6 mm)
round

2 sterling silver tubes, ³⁄₆₄-inch
(1.2 mm) inner diameter,
¼-inch (6 mm) long

Jeweler's saw frame and saw
blades, 0/2 size

Locking tweezers

Steel soldering tripod

Fiber board (used in hot
glass production)

Wire cutters

Round, 20-gauge sterling
silver wire

Paste flux for sterling silver

Butane torch

Jeweler's pickle

Baking soda

Soft wire brush

Round-nose pliers

Instructions

1 Using the ruler and permanent marker, mark a rectangle on the glass ⅝ inches (1.6 cm) wide and 1½ inches (3.8 cm) long. Lay the cork-backed ruler on the sheet of glass, and position it so the wheel of the cutter is on your mark. Score and cut the narrow dimension first. From this strip of glass, score and cut two pieces that are ¾ x 1⅝ inches (1.9 x 4.1 cm). If you've never cut glass before, you may want to practice first. See page 32 for more details on the tools and techniques for glass cutting.

2 Grind the edges of the glass pieces with an alundum stone under a small trickle of running water. You can purchase an alundum stone from an enamel supply store. It's important to always grind glass under running water. The water washes away small chips of glass; otherwise you can damage the surface with cracks or fissures.

3 Use the tissue blade to cut two strips of the sheet clay, ³⁄₁₆ x 4¾ inches (5 mm x 12 cm) each. Cut them on top of the rigid work surface. If you line up the tissue blade the length of the rectangular sheet of clay and press straight down, you'll hear a "snap" when you've cut through. Brush the edge of one of the pieces of glass with water and press the first ¼ inch (6 mm) of the clay sheet onto the glass, and hold to the count of 10. Wrap the rest of the clay sheet around the glass, pressing and adding water as needed to make it stick. Overlap the seam, and cut through both layers with the craft knife. I recommend using a new blade in the craft knife to get a sharp, clean cut. Paint a layer of commercially prepared slip on the seam with the watercolor brush, and set the piece on the hot plate to dry. Repeat this process for the second piece of glass.

4 Use tweezers to lift the pieces from the hot plate. Use the craft knife to trim away the extra paper clay extending past the surface on the front and the back of each piece. If the seam is visible, add more slip to this area.

5 To make the domino graphic pattern, use the paper punch to cut three dots from a piece of sheet clay. Punch a hole in the center of a ⅝-inch (1.6 cm) square of sheet clay. Punch two holes out of one of the ⅝ x ¾ inch (1.6 x 1.9 cm) pieces. Apply these pieces to the glass with a brush of water and position in place (making the domino pattern, with the top side appearing as the reverse of the bottom side). Press lightly with your finger, and count to 10. Repeat this process for the other earring.

Domino Theory

6 Paint the entire back of the pieces with a layer of commercially prepared slip, and let it air dry. Use the watercolor brush to paint all the seams and the corners of the clay-sheet-covered glass with slip and set on the hot plate to dry.

7 Sand the 1 inch (2.5 cm) end of a piece of sterling silver tubing with the coarse emery board. Cut two ¼-inch (6 mm) pieces of tubing using the jeweler's saw frame and saw blade. Clamp a piece of tubing lengthwise with the locking tweezers. Sand a flat wall with the coarse emery board. Be certain to file the entire length of the tubing. This flat spot will provide an area for a strong attachment. Next, you can glue the tubing with commercially prepared slip to the back of the earrings. Hold the tubing in the locking tweezers with the flat side down, and brush the tubing with the slip. Press one tube into place, vertically centered, and ¼ inch (6 mm) down from the top edge of the glass (see photo 1). Repeat for the second earring. Set the earrings on the hot plate to dry the slip before firing.

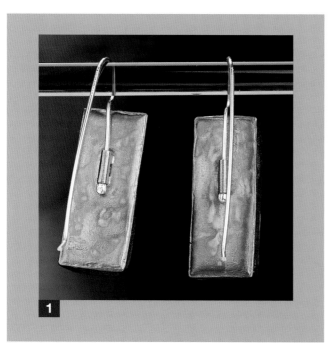

8 Fire at 1200°F (650°C) for 20 minutes with the glass placed face down on top of the fiber board. While firing, you can make the earring wires.

9 Cut two, 3-inch (7.6 cm) pieces of the 20-gauge sterling silver round wire. Dip one end of the wire 1 inch (2.5 cm) into a jar of paste flux, and clamp it into the locking tweezers. Rest the dipped wire on the edge of the soldering tripod. It is important to have the wire perfectly vertical to have professional results. Wait for the flux to dry, and then use the butane torch to heat the end of the wire until the silver balls up. Place the wire in a jeweler's pickle solution until the residue flux and gray oxidation is gone. Rinse well in a solution of baking soda and water to neutralize the pickle. The ratio is about 1 cup (240 ml) of water to 1 tablespoon (15 ml) of baking powder.

10 To finish, use the soft wire brush with soap and water. Burnish in a circular motion. Rinse the piece, and dry well. Thread the sterling silver wire up through the tubing, and bend with round-nose pliers to the earwire shape. Trim away the extra with wire cutters.

Hollow Bead Earrings

Because of the exciting innovations in metal clay, these earrings are as light as they are strong.

Hollow Bead Earrings

Tools & Materials

Metal clay tool kit,
(see page 66)

Two-part silicone mold compound

Four marbles, standard size

Second Generation or Next Generation metal clay, 5 grams

Circular cutter, ¾ inch

Syringe type metal clay

Hot plate

Hole punch, ¼ inch (6 mm)

Sheet metal clay

Support material, such as vermiculite, pearlite, or baking soda

Terra-cotta saucer

Brass wire, 18- or 20-gauge

Rotary tumbler with stainless steel shot and diluted liquid burnishing compound

Glass beads, 8 mm and 6 mm, 2 of each size

Pair of sphere-ended sterling silver headpins

Sterling silver French ear wires

Instructions

1 Follow the manufacturer's directions to mix enough molding compound to hold the four marbles. Push the marbles immediately into the molding compound because it sets quickly. Position them to where each marble is slightly more than halfway covered. Once the mold is set, remove the marbles.

2 Roll out the metal clay to the thickness of three playing cards. Use the circular cutter to cut out four circles that are ¾ inch (1.9 cm) in diameter each. Use your finger to push each of the moist clay circles into one of the concave depressions made in step 1. Let the metal clay dry to bone dry in the mold.

3 Carefully pop the dry clay out of the mold. File the edges flush on all four pieces using the medium side of the coarse emery board. Repeat this until you have four identical domes. On one of the domes, run a line of syringe metal clay around the top edge, then place another dome on top to make a hollow bead. Repeat for the remaining dome shapes.

4 Set the two hollow beads on a hot plate to allow the syringe clay to dry. When dry, file the extra syringe clay away with the fine-grit emery board. Use the coarse emery board to file a crosshatch pattern on the surface to give the bead an interesting texture. You can get this texture by overlapping and changing direction with the emery board as you sand.

5 Punch out four circles from a piece of sheet metal clay with the paper punch. Dip the watercolor brush in water, wipe off most of the water, then dampen the top center of the bead. Set a sheet clay dot on the top center of the bead and press down firmly to secure (see figure 1). Be certain you have a good attachment by checking the

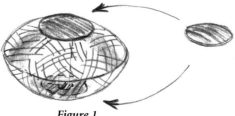

Figure 1

edges all the way around the circle. Repeat this step for the three remaining circles. Set the beads on the hot plate for 1 minute to drive off any remaining moisture.

6 To cut holes in the tops and bottoms of the beads, use the craft knife like a drill. Set the point of the knife in the center of one of the dots and spin it to cut a precise hole. Repeat for the other three holes.

7 To fire, set the beads halfway down in a support material contained in a terra-cotta saucer. Support material could be vermiculite, pearlite, or baking soda. All three can handle the heat of firing, even at 1650°F (900°C) and will act as support for the hollow beads. Otherwise, if you fired the beads directly on a kiln shelf, they would get a flat bottom and/or slump.

8 When the beads have air cooled, thread both on a thin strand of brass wire. Twist the wire to close the loop. Tumble the beads in a rotary tumbler with stainless steel shot and a diluted liquid burnishing compound for 45 minutes. Notice that we skipped the wire brush step, because we want a contrast between the crosshatched surface texture of the silver (matte white), against the highly burnished surface you get from tumbling.

9 Construct the earrings by threading the beads onto the headpins, adding glass beads as adornments, and wire wrapping the ends. Connect the earrings to the sterling silver ear wires.

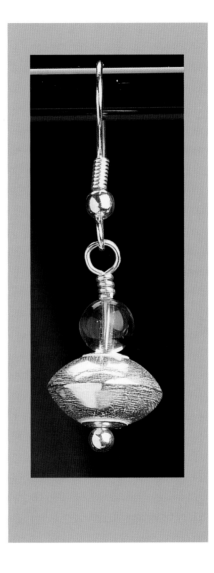

Bauhaus Bold

The use of bold colors in this pin—black, red, and yellow epoxy resin—was inspired by the striking jewelry of 1950s Germany. Be daring. There's a world of color and design possibilities waiting to be explored.

Tools & Materials

Metal clay tool kit, (see page 66)

Sheets of plain paper, 3 x 5 inches (7.6 x 12.7 cm)

Second Generation metal clay, 8.2 grams

Hot plate

Metal clay syringe

Plastic drinking straw, 5 mm in diameter

Coffee mug

Needle-nose jeweler's pliers

Jeweler's saw frame and blades

Ruler with metric and English measurements

Two-part sterling silver pin back with nickel silver pin

Hard silver solder, paste flux, and acetylene torch

Jeweler's pickle solution

Stove top glass pot and baking soda

Wax paper

Industrial-strength, non-yellowing, two-part epoxy

Toothpicks

Powder pigment: yellow, black, and red

Plastic spoon

Craft stick

Shallow plastic dish

1000-grit wet/dry sandpaper

Instructions

1 Begin by making a paper template to achieve the long graceful shape. Fold a 3 x 5 inch (7.6 x 12.7 cm) sheet of plain paper in quarters. Draw a pattern as shown in figure 1. Start ⅜ inch (9.5 mm) from the fold on the narrow side of the folded paper, and draw a curved line down to a point roughly 1¼ inches (3.2 cm) along the longer fold. Cut on the line and unfold. Make two of theses paper templates. Spread olive oil balm on the surface of one of the paper templates.

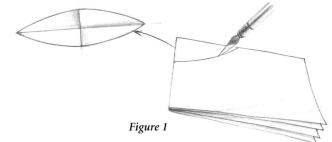

Figure 1

2 On a flexible work surface, roll Second Generation metal clay to the thickness of three playing cards. Set the template on the damp surface of the clay, balm side down. The balm will hold the paper. To cut out the shape, use a thin tissue blade and flex it to fit the curve of the paper template. Cut the clay. Set the form aside to air dry for five minutes, then set it paper-side-down on the hot plate until bone dry (don't worry, the paper will easily come off the dry clay).

3 Roll a length of Second Generation metal clay to mat board thickness, and to at least ½ x 3 inches (1.3 x 7.6 cm). Using the tissue blade, cut down the middle lengthwise. Trim the two new pieces to 4 mm wide each. Place the second paper pattern on a flexible work surface. Stand one strip of clay on edge and shape it to match one edge of the paper pattern. Center this strip so you have an extra ⅛ inch (3 mm) at both ends. This will make one wall of the brooch. Let it dry standing on edge. When this first wall is dry, repeat the steps to make the second wall.

4 Glue one wall to the outside edge of the flat base with syringe clay, and hold the pieces together with firm pressure, and slowly counting to 20. Allow this to dry for 3 minutes before transferring to the hot plate. Remove from the hot plate when the clay is bone dry, and trim away the extra material on the ends with a craft knife. Repeat this step to attach the second wall.

5 Sand the form with the coarse emery board, then use the fine emery board to refine the shape. Add more syringe clay to fill gaps if needed, and let dry. Sand it again, going from the coarse to fine emery boards. Rub a wet wipe over the external walls and edges. This will give a wonderfully smooth surface.

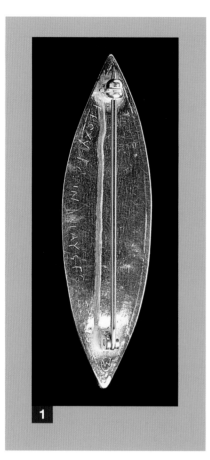

1

6 To finish the design, you'll need to make four more components. Roll out a snake of clay to the thickness of four playing cards. Cut a piece to fit across the lower third of the form. Glue this piece into place with syringe. Use the blender tool to wipe away the extra clay. Set the form on the hot plate to dry.

7 To make the open circle shapes, roll out more clay to the thickness of three playing cards. Use the tissue blade to cut a 1 x ^{13}⁄₁₆ inch (2.5 x 2.1 cm) rectangular shape and wrap it around the plastic drinking straw. Overlap the material and remove the excess with the tissue blade. Knit the seam together with the blender tool. Stand the straw in the coffee mug and allow the clay to air dry. When it's dry, slide the clay tube off the straw. It may be necessary to grip the end of the straw with needle-nose pliers to be able to pull off the metal clay tube. Cut this tubing with a jeweler's saw to make three ³⁄₁₆-inch (5 mm) sections. Glue the circles in place with syringe, and use the blender tool to wipe away the extra syringe. Set the form on the hot plate to dry. When dry, remove the form from the hot plate and sand the top edges with the emery boards, moving from coarse to fine. Keep sanding until no construction seams are visible.

8 Fire for 2 hours at 1650°F (900°C) or any of the suggested firing schedules. Solder the sterling silver two-part pin back to the back of the base with hard solder; (see photo 1). Pickle the piece to neutralize the acid, then boil the piece in a stove top glass pot with 1 tablespoon (15 ml) baking powder and 2 cups (480 ml) of water for 20 minutes. Rinse thoroughly with cold tap water and dry. Set the silver pin and close it with the needle-nose pliers.

9 On a sheet of wax paper, mix the epoxy with toothpicks according to manufacturer's instructions and add powdered pigment to get the desired hue and saturation. Use the plastic spoon to load the epoxy. Push it into the cells with a craft stick to fill each area completely. Set the piece aside to let the epoxy cure. This will take at least 24 hours. If the epoxy layer is thick, it may take a few days to fully cure. For a flush finish, set the brooch facedown in a shallow plastic dish on top of 1000-grit wet/dry sandpaper, and sand until the top is level.

Bead Ring

Prominently showcase a favored lampwork bead by making a ring that puts it on a pedestal for the world to see.

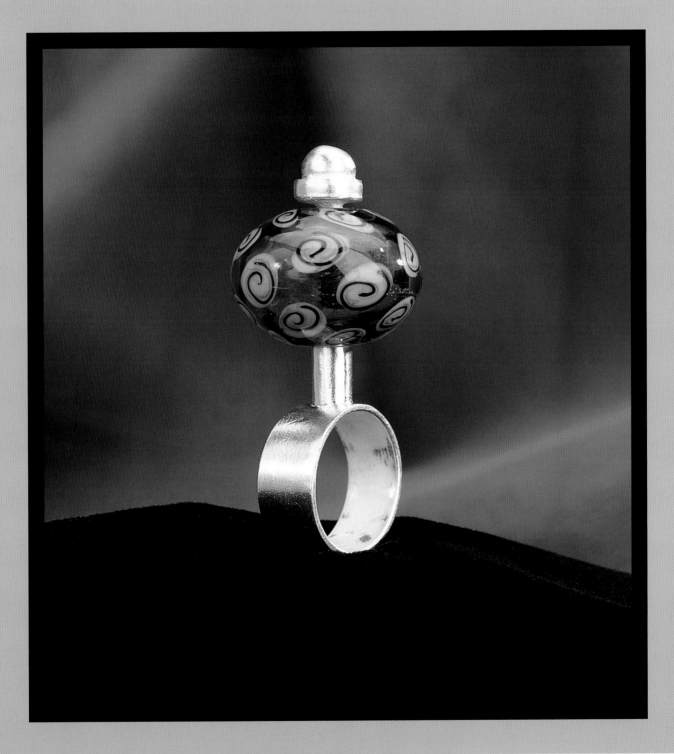

Bead Ring

Tools & Materials

Metal clay tool kit, (see page 66)

Second Generation or Next Generation metal clay, 8 grams

Metric ruler

Calculator

Newspaper

Glue stick

Styrofoam block

Hot plate

Coffee stirrer

Syringe type metal clay

Stainless steel bolts, 2 (to fit hole and depth of bead)

Terra-cotta saucer filled with vermiculite

Handcrafted bead

Instructions

1 Determine the ring size you wish to make and calculate for the metal clay shrinkage. Use the guide on page 140 as a worksheet for making these calculations.

2 Next, make a newspaper mandrel to fit your ring length (from step 3 of the worksheet used to calculate step 1). Cut a long strip of newspaper 1 inch (2.5 cm) in width, and wrap it around the handle end of the needle tool. Continue adding to the strip of newspaper until it matches the sizing strip from step 1. Use the glue stick to secure the end of the newspaper.

3 Roll out the clay to the thickness of four playing cards, and slightly longer than the paper pattern. Use the tissue blade to cut the clay to your desired width. Wrap the metal clay around the newspaper mandrel, and overlap at the seam. Using the tissue blade, cut through both layers at an angle, then close the seam with the blender tool. Set the clay band aside to dry to leather hard (not quite bone dry). The ring will come off the newspaper coil by pulling away the pin tool (from the center). The inside will unravel like a Chinese yo-yo. This will not put pressure on the ring, which is very fragile at this stage. Place the ring on a hot plate to dry to bone dry.

4 You may notice a lot of little cracks on the edges. This is typical with these clay formulas. File the edges and the seam with the fine emery board until all the cracks are gone. Use a wet wipe to further refine the sides until you have nice smooth edges. The band part of the ring is complete.

5 The part that holds the bead to the ring is a length of threaded metal clay tubing. It sounds hard, but it isn't. Roll out a slab of clay to the thickness of three playing cards. Cut a ⅝ x ¾-inch (1.6 cm x 1.9 cm) piece and wrap it around the end of the coffee stirrer. Cut the seam with the tissue blade to make a butt joint (where the edges are flush against each other). Use the No. 0 blending tool to close the seam. Add some metal clay syringe if necessary to close the seam. Set on the hot plate to dry. When it's dry, slide it off the straw, and file the edges. Twist one of the bolts slowly into the tubing. Complete only one turn, then back it out. Twist the bolt into the clay for two complete turns, and back the bolt out

again. Each revolution will cut into the walls of the metal clay, threading the tubing. Repeat until you have cut a thread through the entire ½-inch-length (1.3 cm) of tubing. Decorate the end of the other bolt with metal clay. (I completely covered the end of the bolt by using the syringe and then sculpted the shapes with a damp brush.) Set this piece on the hot plate to dry.

6 To attach the tubing to the ring shank, cut a hole in the ring band by using the craft knife like a drill. Cut the hole to match the inside diameter of the tubing. Attach the tubing to the ring with syringe, and wipe away the extra with the blender tool. Set on the hot plate to dry.

7 Gently screw the bolt into the tubing, and fire with the bolt end buried in vermiculite. The ring will be on top and the bolt on the bottom, upside down. Fire at 1650°F (900°C) for 10 minutes. When the piece is cool, you can twist the bolt out. It may be stubborn at first, but it will unscrew. The steel will not fuse to the fine silver, so it is possible to fire the pieces together.

8 I decided to contrast the glossy bead with a soft satin finish. To create this effect, wire brush the ring components with soap and water, dry well, and attach the glass bead with the decorated screw. This bead can be interchanged with other beads with the same opening diameter (see figure 1). You can proudly display a different bead every day of the week with this interchangeable ring.

Figure 1

Cherry Blossoms in Spring

A colleague showed me his method of creating collages with metal clay and glass. It inspired me to try the same technique on enameled surfaces.

Tools & Materials

Metal clay tool kit, (see page 66)

Second Generation metal clay

Playing cards

Rubber stamp, botanical print

Hot plate

Sheet metal clay, rectangular size

Pair of craft sticks

Brass tubing, size ⅜ and ⁵⁄₃₂ inch (9.5 and 3.9 mm)

Commercially prepared slip

Pair of kiln blocks

Kiln shelf

Sandpaper for wood, 60-grit

Rotary tumbler, mixed stainless steel shot, and liquid burnishing compound

Paper towels

Transparent enamel, Elan gray, and blue-black

Steel trivet for enameling

Kiln fork

Heat-resistant surface

Blue-gray opaque enamel

Burnishing tool

Sakura (cherry blossom) decorative paper punches, 15 and 11.5 mm

Soft brass brush

2 sterling silver jump rings, 4.4 mm

Silk cord, sterling silver chain, or ribbon for hanging

Instructions

1 Roll out the metal clay to the thickness of four playing cards. Press the botanical print rubber stamp into the surface of the clay. Cut a 2½ x 1½-inch (6.4 x 3.8 cm) rectangular shape out of the slab of clay using a tissue blade. Set the wet side (the plain side with no texture) faceup on the hot plate to dry.

2 When the piece is bone dry, remove it from the hot plate with tweezers, and sand the edges with the coarse emery board. Sand the corners and round them slightly.

3 Use the tissue blade to cut two pieces from the sheet metal clay that measure ⅛ x 4½ inch (3 mm x 12 cm). Dampen one side of the strip of sheet clay, and wrap it around the edge of the large slab of bone-dry clay. As you wrap, position the sheet clay in the center of the edge of the slab, leaving a 1 mm edge on each side. Set this piece on its edge with the long side of the rectangle on the hot plate to dry.

4 To make the bails (hanging devices), roll out a marble-size ball of clay to the thickness of the craft sticks. Cut two circles from the slab of moist clay with ⅜-inch (9.5 mm) brass tubing. Cut the centers out with the smaller brass tubing. Set these pieces on the hot plate to dry. When these circles are bone dry, take them off the hot plate using tweezers so you don't burn your fingers. Sand a ⅛-inch (3 mm) flat edge on both circles with the coarse emery board. Use the commercially prepared slip like glue to attach circles to the top of the piece (see photo 1, page 90). Set the pendant on the hot plate to dry the slip.

5 When the slip is dry, fire the piece at 1650°F (900°C) for 20 minutes. Support the piece in the center (with a kiln block lying flat on a kiln shelf) so you don't collapse the paper clay edge. Sand a second kiln block with the sandpaper until it fits under the bails. If you don't support them, they'll slump in the firing.

6 After firing (and when cool), tumble for 45 minutes in a rotary tumbler with mixed stainless steel shot and a diluted solution of liquid burnishing compound. Hold by the edges and rinse under running water. Pat dry with a paper towel. Enamel the stamp-textured side with an ⅛-inch (3 mm) sifting of transparent enamel.

Cherry Blossoms in Spring

1

7 Carefully set the piece on a steel trivet. Set the trivet on a kiln shelf. Set the shelf, trivet, and pendant in a 1700°F (927°C) heated kiln. When you open the kiln door, the temperature will drop to 1500°F (816°C). Fire for 3 minutes at this temperature. Remove the trivet and pendant from the kiln using the kiln fork, place it on a heat-resistant surface, and allow it to cool. Flip the piece to the other side and sift an ⅛-inch (3 mm) layer of opaque blue-black enamel onto the surface. Fire the piece as before to fuse the enamel to the surface.

8 Use a burnishing tool to hand polish the bails and the sides of the pendant. Then use the burnishing tool to fold over the paper clay in a scalloping fashion on both sides. The paper clay will act as a bezel to visually frame the pendant and protect the enamel surface at the edges from chipping or cracking. The finished bezel will resemble a pie crust.

9 Use the paper punches to punch out one large and four small cherry blossoms from a scrap piece of sheet clay (these cherry blossom punches are available from several metal clay suppliers). Cut two of the smaller cherry blossoms with a tissue blade to create an interesting pattern. Attach the sheet clay pieces with a brush of water to the opaque enamel side of the pendant. Use the watercolor brush and paint some commercially prepared slip between the decorations. Add water to fuzz the edges of the slip with the watercolor brush (this is similar to a technique used in watercolor painting). You can add water or slip to get a pattern that you like. If you don't like the surface design, you can use a wet wipe to clean the surface and start over. Once the pattern is to your liking, set on the hot plate to dry.

10 Set the pendant back on the enameling trivet (that's sitting on a kiln shelf). Fire at 1200°F (649°C) for 10 minutes. This will fire the sheet clay and fuse the fine silver to the enamel.

11 Use the soft wire brush with liquid soap and water to finish the metal surface. Add the jump rings and attach a coordinating cord of your choice for a wonderfully wearable necklace.

A Day at the Beach Bracelet

Use the different shrinkage rates of metal clay to your advantage. By mixing formulas of clay, you can easily create graduated sizes of the same molded shape.

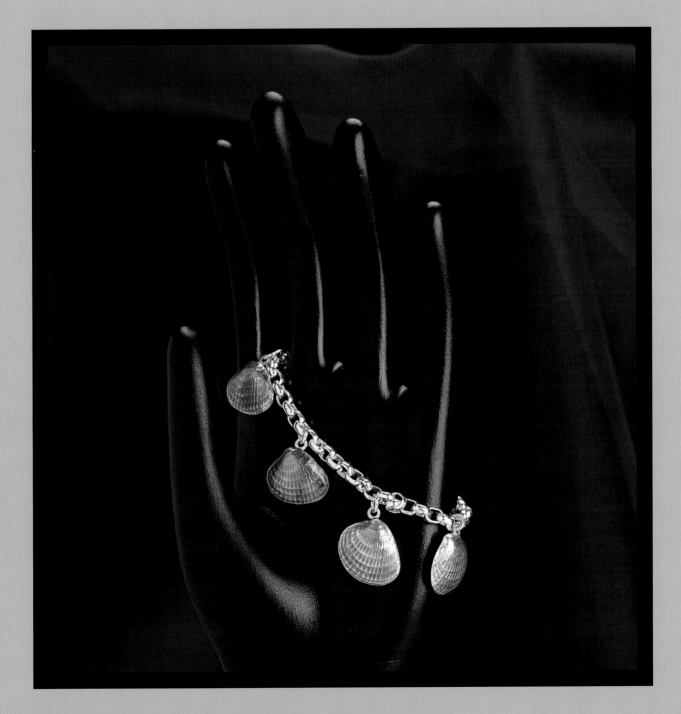

A Day at the Beach Bracelet

Tools & Materials

Metal clay tool kit,
  (see page 66)

Seashell

Two-part silicone molding
  material

First Generation metal clay,
  13 grams

Next Generation metal clay,
  12 grams

Jeweler's gram scale

Silver tabs made of 950 silver
  alloy

Hot plate

Kiln shelf

Rotary tumbler, stainless steel
  shot, and a diluted liquid
  burnishing compound

Binding agent

Distilled water

Transparent enamel powder,
  6 different colors

80-mesh enamel sifter

Flat-nose jewelry pliers, 2 pairs

Sterling silver jump rings,
  3.2 mm, 18-gauge wire

Sterling silver linked bracelet

Instructions

1 Make a mold of a seashell using the two-part molding material. Follow the manufacturer's directions and mix enough molding compound to hold the shell. Push the shell halfway down into the mold material.

2 When the mold has set, pop the seashell out. Press a small ball of First Generation metal clay into the mold. Use your thumb to hollow out a depression in the back. This will make the piece weigh less (and more economical). Use a tissue blade to trim away the extra clay. Flex out the moist clay from the mold directly onto a gram scale to get the weight (mine weighed 4 grams).

3 Next, mix combinations of First and Next Generation metal clay to create each of the six shells. Use the guide below to mix metal clay for each. By using these hybrids, you'll create a group of pieces that are different sizes, but all pulled from the same mold. The bracelet featured in this project has six different sizes, but you can make many more:

Metal Clay Mixing Guide

	First Generation	mixed with	Next Generation
Shell 1	4 grams		0 grams
Shell 2	3 grams		1 gram
Shell 3	2.5 grams		1.5 grams
Shell 4	2 grams		2 grams
Shell 5	1 gram		3 grams
Shell 6	0 grams		4 grams

4 While the clay is still moist, push a 950 silver alloy tab in the topside of all six of the metal clay shells. Place all the pieces on a hot plate to dry to bone dry.

5 Refine the shell edges using the emery boards, starting with the coarse grit, moving to the fine grit. Fire all the clay pieces flat on a kiln shelf at 1650°F (900°C) for 2 hours. Whenever you combine different clay formulas, you need to fire for the longest firing schedule for the formulas you are using.

6 When the shells have cooled, they're ready to be polished. Brush the shells with a wire brush with soap and water, then place them in a rotary tumbler with stainless steel shot and a diluted liquid burnishing compound. Tumble the shells for 45 minutes.

7 Remove the pieces from the tumbler by carefully holding their edges. While still holding by the edges, rinse well with clean water, dry with a paper towel, and set aside for the enameling step. You don't want to touch the top of the pieces with your fingers because the oils from your hand will cause the enamel to resist adhering to the metal.

8 Lift the shells with tweezers, gripping by the silver tab, and brush the molded side (or the side with the texture you want featured) with a binding solution that's equal parts binding agent and distilled water. Sift the shells with a 2 mm layer of enamel from the sifter. Set on a kiln shelf, and place on top of the kiln. Allow the enamel to dry completely.

9 Preheat the kiln to 1500°F (816°C). Place the kiln shelf in the kiln for about 3 minutes. Fire each shell independently. Because each enamel color has its own fusing point, this amount of time is given here simply as a general guide. When the surface is clear and glassy, remove it from the kiln and let the shell air cool. Repeat for the five remaining pieces. If you use analogous colors (referring to colors that appear next to each other on a color wheel, for example yellow-green, green, blue/green, blue, blue-violet) it will emphasize the graduation in sizes.

10 Use two pairs of flat-nose jewelry pliers and jump rings to attach the charms to the linked bracelet.

950 Silver Alloy Tabs

I recommend you use 950 silver alloy tabs as inserts for this project. Sterling silver tabs (made of 925 sterling silver) will melt in the intense heat of firing. Silver alloy tabs are made to withstand high firing temperatures. You can find them at most metal clay retailers and suppliers.

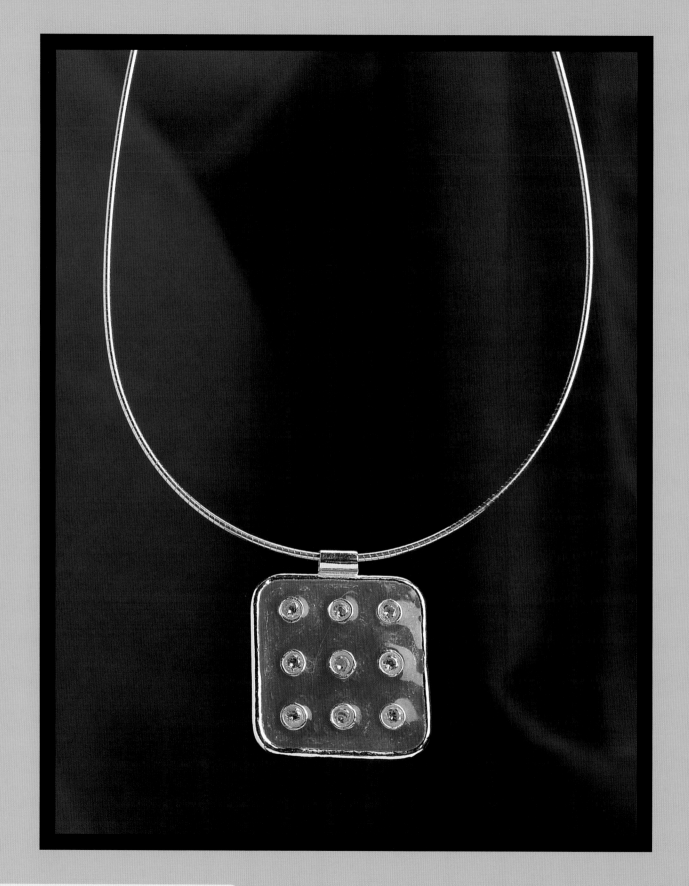

Bejeweled
Pendant

This piece was inspired by a love for all things Tiffany and Fabergé. Diamonds, rubies, emeralds, and sapphires were used with sinfully rich transparent enameled surfaces.

Tools & Materials

Metal clay tool kit,
  (see page 66)

Second Generation metal clay,
  12 grams

Hot plate

Pair of craft sticks

Brass plunger-style cutter,
  5 mm diameter

Coffee stirrer, 3 mm diameter

Syringe metal clay

Flexible shaft with 3 mm stone
  cutting bur

9 yellow cubic zironia stones,
  3 mm round

Kiln shelf

Rotary tumbler, stainless
  steel shot, and burnishing
  solution

80-mesh transparent enamel

Binding agent

Distilled water

Plastic spoon

High-quality watercolor brush,
  size No. 1

Steel trivet

Heat-resistant gloves

Kiln fork, or long-handled
  spatula

Sterling silver, round cable-
  style necklace

Instructions

1 Roll out the clay to the thickness of three playing cards. Cut a 1¼-inch (3.2 cm) square with the tissue blade. Set on the hot plate to dry. When the piece is bone dry, file the sides, and round the corners by using the emery boards. Start with the coarse board, and finish with the fine.

2 Roll out a coil of clay 5½ inches (14 cm) long, and 2 mm in diameter. Brush the edge of the rounded square with a generous amount of water, and attach the coil of clay to the edge. Blend the seam with the blender tool, and set the piece back on the hot plate to dry.

3 Roll out a thick slab of clay to the thickness of the craft sticks. Cut nine plugs from this slab using the brass cutter. Set the moist plugs on the square in a grid pattern, and attach them with a brush of water. Dry on the hot plate.

4 To make the bail, roll out a marble-size piece of metal clay to the thickness of one playing card. Cut a ¼ x 1 inch (6 mm x 2.5 cm) strip of clay, and wrap it around a 3 mm coffee stirrer. Overlap and cut the seam with the tissue blade. Blend the seam with the blender tool and set the piece on the hot plate to dry. When the piece is bone dry, it will slide off the straw. Sand the edges of the bail with the fine emery file, and glue in place with syringe clay. Reinforce the bail's seam on the back with more syringe clay and blend it into the back with a damp brush. Set the pendant on the hot plate to drive off the moisture.

5 Using the craft knife, drill a hole in the exact center of each plug. Then, using the flex shaft and a 3 mm stone setting bur, cut a seat in the center of each plug to hold the stones. The plugs will act as bezels to hold the stones in place after firing. Keep checking the fit of the stone in the hole you're cutting. The table of stone needs to sit ⅛ inch (3 mm) below the rim of the plug for a tension fit (see page 57).

Bejeweled Pendant

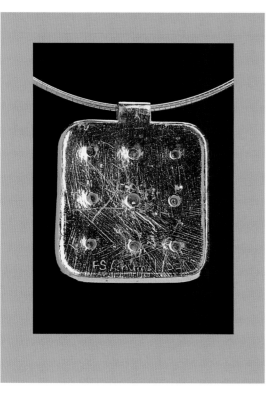

6 After setting all the stones, carefully inspect the fit, then fire the piece flat on a kiln shelf for 2 hours at 1650°F (900°C). For enameling, it's recommended to use the longest firing schedule to get the densest metal possible.

7 Tumble the pendant for 45 minutes in a rotary tumbler with a burnishing solution and stainless steel shot. If this seems like a long time to tumble a piece of metal clay, you're right. From the kiln, metal clay has a porous surface. It's not a good surface for enameling. Tumbling will burnish the pores closed.

8 Mix the powdered enamel with a 50/50 solution of binding agent and distilled water. Use a high-quality watercolor brush and a plastic spoon to position the enamel onto the metal clay surface. This technique is known as wet packing (see page 65).

9 Rest the piece on a steel trivet, and place the trivet on a kiln shelf. Set the shelf on top of a hot kiln to dry. When the enamel is completely dry, wear your heat-resistant gloves and load the piece into the hot kiln using either the kiln fork or long-handled spatula. The temperature needs to be 2000°F (1093°C). As soon as you open the door, the temperature will drop dramatically. Close the door when the pyrometer reads 1500°F (816°C) and set a kitchen timer for 3 minutes. Check the piece by opening the door to see if the enamel surface is even and glassy. If not, close the door and set the timer for 2 minutes more.

10 Allow the pendant to cool. Tumble it again for 20 minutes for a high polish finish. Hang from a sterling silver round cable-style necklace.

Falling Leaves

Instead of simply repeating a pattern, try evoking the idea of movement. Lead the eye around the piece, link by link, by slightly changing the position of a key design element. Think of each link as a frame in a jewelry movie.

Falling Leaves

Tools & Materials

Metal clay tool kit,
(see page 66)

Index card, 3 x 5 inches (7.6
x 12.7 cm)

Corner punch

Second Generation metal
clay, 32 grams

Hot plate

Ruler

Sheet metal clay, 2 sheets of
the long rectangle size

Mechanical pencil with

Commercially prepared slip

Fine mist spray bottle

Paper punch, ⅛ inch (3 mm)

Kiln shelf

Flexible shaft, ¹⁄₁₆ inch (1.6
mm) metal-cutting drill bit,
drill bit lubricant

Rotary-style tumbler, mixed
stainless steel shot, and
liquid burnishing
compound

80-mesh enamel sifter

Transparent enamel powder

21 medium sterling silver
jump rings 18-gauge,
5 mm

Flat-nose pliers, 2 pair

Sterling silver tube clasp,
1¼ inches (3.2 cm) long

Instructions

1 Cut a 1¼ x 1¼ inch (3.2 x 3.2 cm) square template from the index card. Punch out the rounded the corners with a corner punch. If you don't have a corner punch, trace the rounded edge from a playing card and use a craft knife to cut all four corners of your template. Draw a leaf shape in the center of the template, and cut it out with a craft knife. Be sure your craft knife has a sharp new blade.

2 Roll out an entire package of Second Generation metal clay on a flexible work surface to the thickness of three playing cards. Use a pin tool and the template to cut out six solid bracelet panels. Let the pieces dry for 5 minutes before transferring them to the hot plate with the wet side of the clay facing up.

3 After the pieces are bone dry, remove them from the hot plate. Stack all six pieces on top of one another and file with the coarse emery board until they are perfectly matched. Pay close attention to the rounded corners. After filing, they should measure ¹³⁄₁₆ inches (3 cm).

4 Sheet metal clay comes in a square or long rectangle. For this project you will need two sheets of the rectangular version. First, using one sheet, the ruler, and craft knife, cut four squares, each measuring ¹³⁄₁₆ inches (3 cm). Set three of these aside for use in step 6. On the remaining square, trace three leaf shapes using the mechanical pencil and template. Use a craft knife with a brand new blade to cut out the leaves (save and use the leftover sheet clay from this step for the dots you punch in step 8). With the second piece of sheet clay, cut three long strips measuring ⅛ x 4¹¹⁄₁₆ inches (3 mm x 11.9 cm).

5 Brush one square panel (from step 2) generously with water. Position one sheet clay leaf cutting from step 4 onto the panel, and attach by pressing lightly with your finger. To finish the edges, brush them with water, then wrap one long strip (cut in step 4) around the edge of the panel. The strip is long enough that it will overlap slightly. Cut away the extra using the craft knife to get an exact fit and close the seam with a brush of commercially prepared slip. Set this piece on the hot plate to dry. Repeat this step for the other two panels so that you have three pieces with applied leaves.

6 Lay the leaf template on one of the sheet clay squares (from the three left from step 4). With the mechanical pencil, trace the leaf shape so that it is centered on the sheet. Cut out the leaf shape with the craft knife. Flip to the backside of the template and repeat this for the next sheet clay square. Turn the template 180°, trace and then cut out the leaf shape on the last sheet clay square. You should now have three sheet clay squares with the leaf pattern pierced out of the center, all with a different orientation.

Figure 1

7 Attach the sheet clay to the panels by generously misting the panels with water, using a fine mist spray bottle. Adhere the sheet by pressing lightly with your finger. Work from the center out to the edge. Be sure to work out any trapped air bubbles. Do this for all three panels. Set them on the hot plate to dry. When bone dry, place facedown on a cutting surface and trim the extra sheet clay from the rounded corners with the craft knife. Smooth the edges by rubbing them with a wet wipe until no seam is showing from laminating the sheet clay to the panel.

8 Each panel will have six holes drilled into the piece after firing. The three holes on each side will accommodate the jump rings. Because of the enameled background, it is important to reinforce each hole with metal because enamel alone could crack or chip with wear. Use the ⅛ inch (3 mm) paper punch to make 36 small circles. Attach the sheet clay dots to each panel with a brush of water. Place the clay dots ⅛ inch (3 mm) from the outside edge of each panel (see figure 1). Set each panel on the hot plate to dry. When they're bone dry, use the pin tool to place a dimple in the center of each sheet clay dot. Don't try to poke through; you need to just make a mark in the clay. The holes will be drilled out after firing, and this center marking will hold the drill bit in place.

9 Lay the six finished panels on a kiln shelf and fire for 2 hours at 1650°F (900°C). For enameling, you will want the strongest, densest material possible, and this long firing time will do the trick. After firing, use the flexible shaft and the 1/16 inch (1.6 mm) drill bit (with lubricant) to drill six holes in each panel. Brush the piece with the wire brush and soap and water. Tumble the pieces for 45 minutes in a rotary tumbler with stainless steel shot and a burnishing compound.

Falling Leaves

10 Apply the enamel. For the three applied leaf panels, use the mesh sifter to dry sift the enamel over the entire piece, using a dry watercolor brush to brush the excess enamel off the leaves. Use the wet packing technique (see page 65) to fill the recessed leaves on the other three panels. When the enamel is thoroughly dry, set the pieces on a kiln shelf and load them into a kiln preheated to 2000°F (1093°C). The temperature will drop when you open the door and the enamel will fuse in about 3 minutes at 1500°F (816°C). This is only a general guide because each color of enamel will fuse at a different temperature. When the surface of the enamel is glassy, remove the kiln shelf from the kiln and set on a heat resistant surface. Allow the pieces to air cool.

11 To assemble, use the sterling silver jump rings to link the panels of the bracelet. Open the jump rings by gripping lightly with two flat-nose pliers and twisting from side to side. Slide on two adjacent panels before closing the jump rings by twisting closed. Attach a commercial sterling silver tube clasp (see photo 1).

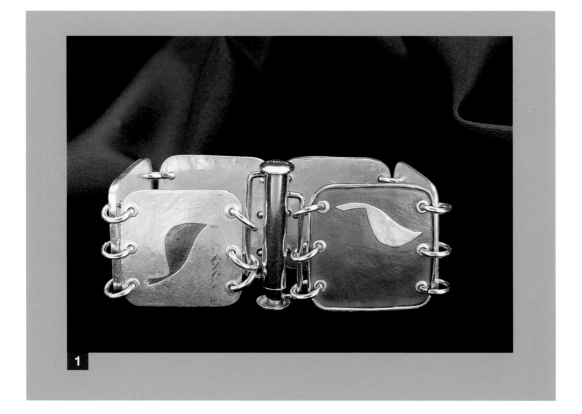

Bamboo Garden

The Asian theme of this pendant was inspired by using a Japanese watercolor brush. In fact, I used one to apply the wax resist for this water-etched design. Creating a relief by wiping away clay is a simple technique that yields beautiful results.

Bamboo Garden

Metal clay tool kit,
(see page 66)

Tools & Materials

Metal clay tool kit,
(see page 66)

Second Generation metal
clay, 14 grams

Pair of craft sticks

Hot plate

Nail polish and nail polish
remover

Plastic texture sheet

Kiln shelf

Drill bit, No. 56 size and
rotary tool

Rotary tumbler with mixed
stainless steel shot and
liquid burnishing com-
pound

80-mesh enamel sifter

Transparent enamel

Enameling spatula

Pair of sterling silver jump
rings, 18-gauge (3.2 mm)

Sterling silver cable-style
necklace

Instructions

1 Roll out Second Generation metal clay to the thickness of the craft sticks, then cut a free-hand rectangle 1½ x 1⅜ inches (3.8 x 3.4 cm) with the pin tool. The thicker the slab of clay, the better for this technique. The clay will give a deeper relief surface, thus a more dramatic effect. Place the piece on a hot plate to dry. When bone dry, use nail polish and the watercolor brush to paint a design on the dry clay surface, and let the nail polish dry completely. Clean the watercolor brush with nail polish remover.

2 Rub a wet wipe over the surface of the clay. The wipe will pick up the silver clay wherever it's exposed; this area will be "etched" away. The areas covered with the nail polish will resist the etching process and stay at the original height (craft stick thickness). Continue etching until the desired depth is reached. If the slab of metal clay gets overly wet and mushy, stop. Let the metal clay air dry to bone dry, then continue etching.

3 To make the backing piece, roll out more Second Generation metal clay on top of the plastic texture sheet to the thickness of three playing cards. Use a texture with a low profile. For deeper textures, you'll need to roll out a thicker slab of metal clay. Set the etched piece on top of the textured slab. Use the pin tool to cut a rectangle that's slightly larger than the etched piece. Dry the piece on the hot plate to bone dry. Refine the edges on both pieces using the emery board.

4 Fire both pieces flat on a kiln shelf at 1650°F (900°C) for 10 minutes.

5 After the pieces have cooled, drill two holes at the top of both pieces with the drill bit. Wire brush with soap and water to get a satin finish. Tumble for 45 minutes to 1 hour. Remove the pieces from the tumbler with tweezers and rinse well with clean water (using the tweezers to hold the piece). Dry the piece with a paper towel and set aside for the enameling step.

6 Review the information about enameling on page 64 before you start. Use the enamel sifter to dust a ⅛-inch (3 mm) layer of pale-colored, transparent enamel on the etched piece. For the back piece, dust a ¹⁄₁₆-inch (1.6 mm) layer of a darker color of enamel. Carefully lay each piece on a kiln shelf. Don't disturb the enamel powder or allow any to spill. A small metal spatula is useful for moving the enameled pieces.

7 Preheat the kiln to 1500°F (816°C). Place the kiln shelf in the hot kiln for about 3 minutes. This amount of time is a general guide, because each enamel color has its own fusing point. When the surface is clear and glassy on both pieces, remove from the kiln and let air cool.

8 Attach the two panels with the jump rings and thread through a length of sterling silver cable-style necklace.

Autumn Dragonfly

The technique in this piece focuses on using metal clay slip on top of fine silver mesh as a foundation for plique-á-jour enameling.

Tools & Materials

Metal clay tool kit,
  (see page 66)

Pencil and paper

Pair of clear plastic page
  protectors

2 pieces of fine silver mesh,
  2¹¹⁄₃₂ square

Syringe metal clay

Hot plate

Solder cutting shears, or
  sharp kitchen shears

Kiln shelf

Set of jeweler's needle files

Next Generation metal clay,
  2 grams

Craft stick spacers

Brass tubing cutter,
  ⅝ inch (1.6 cm)

Small terra-cotta pot filled
  with vermiculite

Enamel colors: chartreuse,
  raspberry, and pink

Distilled water

Binding agent

Plastic spoon

High-quality watercolor brush,
  size No. 0

Steel mesh firing screen

20-gauge steel binding wire

Flat-nose pliers

Kiln fork

Crystal beads: (3) 7 mm
  round, (1) 5 mm round,
  (4) 6 mm faceted,
  (4) 4 mm faceted

Sterling silver round wire,
  20-gauge

Round-nose pliers

Silk ribbon (optional)

Instructions

1 Draw a pattern for the dragonfly wings on a sheet of paper (see figure 1). Slip the paper pattern into the document sleeve. Place the silver mesh on top of the pattern. You'll be able to make one side of the wings from one square piece of mesh. Hold the syringe 1 inch (2.5 cm) above the silver mesh, extrude the slip, and trace the pattern of the wings. This technique is successful if you let the coil of silver drop as it comes from the tip of the syringe. Have gravity work for you. Flip the mesh over. While you're holding it in the air, paint a generous brush of water on the back side along the syringe line. This will help bond the metal clay to the fine silver mesh. Set the piece—syringe-side-up—on the hot plate to dry. Repeat this process to make a second pair of wings.

2 Repeat step 1 on the back side of the mesh by adding a coil of syringe. Paint water along the bottom edge of the syringe for a strong attachment to the silver clay from the front side. Set on the hot plate to dry. Repeat this with the other wing.

3 Cut the wings out of the mesh with the solder cutting shears, or sharp kitchen shears, leaving a ⅛-inch border from the syringe. Fire both pieces (lying flat) on a kiln shelf at 1650°F (900°C) for 20 minutes. The syringe clay will shrink and attach to the fine silver mesh. Use the shears to trim the wings out of the mesh. File the edges smooth with a needle file.

4 To attach the wings, you'll need to make a connector piece. Roll out a pea-size ball of metal clay to craft stick thickness. Cut a circle out of the moist clay with the brass tubing cutter. Use the needle tool to poke a hole in the center of the clay. Set this piece on the hot plate to dry. When bone dry, carve two notches (one on each side of the disk) with the craft knife. Fit the wings in the notches and glue them into place with syringe clay (see photo 1, next page). Don't wipe away the extra syringe that squishes out. You will need this extra material to hold the wings in place during firing. While the syringe clay is still moist, carefully place the construction vertically in a terra-cotta pot, and fill with vermiculite.

Figure 1

Autumn Dragonfly

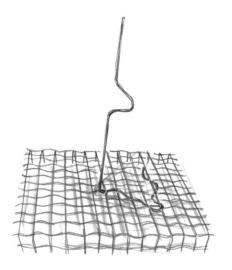

Figure 2

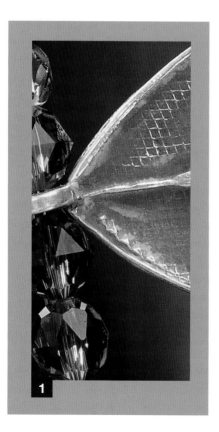

5 Fire the clay pot at 1650°F (900°C) for 2 hours to assure a strong bond. When the piece has cooled, use the needle files to refine the joint.

6 Lay the wings on a clean piece of clear plastic document sleeve. Pack wet enamel into the wings, using at least two different colors. Use a plastic spoon and a good quality watercolor brush to wet-pack the enamel colors on the silver mesh (see page 65). You may notice the red and pink colors are more in the orange tones. Certain colors of enamel will react when in direct contact with silver. Make small samples on fired pieces of metal clay to test your enamel colors. I make simple stud earrings to use as test pieces. If everything works, I can use them as extra jewelry pieces.

7 Attach a piece of steel binding wire to the steel mesh firing screen. Bend a kink in the wire with the flat-nose pliers and attach the wings so they'll stand vertically on the wire (see figure 2). Thread the wings onto the stand. Be certain the enamel is thoroughly dry. Fire in a hot kiln (1500° to 1700°F [815°C to 927°C]) for 3 minutes. Remove the piece using the kiln fork. Don't be surprised if there are some holes in the wings. This is to be expected. When the piece has cooled, wet-pack the holes and fire again. It may take up to three times to fill the wings perfectly.

8 String the crystal beads onto the sterling silver wire. Start with the 4 mm faceted beads, then add the 6 mm faceted beads, then two of the 7 mm round beads. Place the wings onto the wire, then add the last 7 mm bead. Top the dragonfly figure with the 5 mm round bead. Bend the wire with round-nose pliers to make a fibula-style pin. The pin could also be hung from a silk ribbon and worn as a pendant. If you'd like to try a different design, one that's more intricate and challenging, try altering the wing design as shown in figure 3.

Figure 3

Child's Cuff Bracelet

Carving into dry metal clay is incredibly rewarding. This piece combines the wide-open possibilities of this new material with more traditional metal-forming techniques.

Child's Cuff Bracelet

Tools & Materials

Metal clay tool kit,
(see page 66)

Next Generation metal clay,
40 grams

Pair of craft sticks

Flexible work surface

Hot plate

Cardstock

Graph paper

Cork-backed steel ruler,
6 inch (15.2 cm)

Carving tools

Kiln shelf

Steel bracelet mandrel

Rawhide mallet

Instructions

1 Calculate how long to make the bracelet to compensate for the shrinkage rate of Next Generation metal clay. There are two calculation methods described in this book: One is to follow a general sizing chart; the other is to do the math for a custom fit (see the Cuff-Style Bracelet Sizing Chart on page 140). This project was made to fit a child, so I started with a length of 5¼ inches (13.2 cm). To make a bracelet to fit my wrist, I'd use the custom fit formula. Plug your own numbers into the blanks to make a custom-fit bracelet.

2 Roll a slab of clay to craft stick thickness on top of a flexible work sheet. Use a tissue blade and cut a ¾-inch-wide (1.9 cm) strip of clay to the length you calculated in step 1. Allow the piece to air dry for 1 hour. Don't force dry yet, because quick drying a thick slab of clay will promote cracking. After an hour, move it to a hot plate.

3 While the piece is drying, you can make a carving template out of graph paper glued onto cardstock. Draw the pattern and cut it out with a fresh blade in the craft knife. I use a 6-inch cork-backed ruler to reduce the risk of the ruler slipping as I'm cutting. If you prefer, you can draw the pattern directly on the dry slab of clay. For me, it was easier to get an accurate repetitive pattern by using the graph paper.

4 Transfer the pattern to the bone-dry slab and use the carving tools to create the design. If you have not carved in metal clay before, I suggest you practice first to build confidence. I love working the clay this way, and every time I carve into the surface of metal clay, I wonder why I don't use this technique more often.

5 Use coarse then fine emery boards to file the edges of the carved slab. Use the fine-grit emery board to file a 45° beveled edge. (This is important to do well, because the beveled edge will get a high polish after firing.) When the edges are refined to your liking, set the piece flat on a kiln shelf and fire at 1650°F (900°C) for 2 hours (extra time for added strength). You'll shape the bracelet after firing.

6 Let the piece cool, then wire brush it with soap and water. Dry thoroughly. Shape the fired metal over a steel bracelet mandrel, striking the piece with a rawhide mallet. You don't want the metal to be damp or wet because moisture will ruin the surface of the mandrel. Rawhide won't leave a mark the way a metal hammer would. Start at the ends of the cuff and alternate sides, working toward the center. Check the fit, then continue.

7 For a high-contrast finish, jewelers often use a jet black patina that is sold under a couple different names. I don't like to use this type of chemical because it has a skull and crossbones on the label and comes with its own Materials Safety Data Sheet (MSDS). I bypass that mess by using what I call the "marker patina." I use a fine-tip permanent black marker to get the lines nice and black, and touch-up is easy (see photo 1). Create more visual depth by rubbing the edges by hand with the burnisher.

1

Conditioning Your Mallet

Here's a tip for new mallets: a brand new rawhide mallet needs to be beat up to make it nice and soft. Rawhide is saturated in lacquer and until you soften the ends of the mallet, it will leave a mark. I took my brand new hammer out to the sidewalk and started whacking away until the ends were soft (also called "conditioned"). My neighbors already think I'm nuts anyway.

Golden Ivy

The pattern for this piece was inspired by a humble doodle. The formula of gold metal clay used has the same shrinkage rate as the newest form of its silver counterpart—a distinct design advantage.

Tools & Materials

Metal clay tool kit, (see page 66)

Next Generation metal clay, 32 grams

Cardstock to make template

Hot plate

Carving tool

22-karat gold clay, 1.7 grams

Firm tip blender tool

Ultra-fine sponge sanding pad

Sheet form of metal clay, rectangle shape, 4 pieces

Nonstick baking sheet or ironing pad, 2 pieces at least 5 inches (12.7 cm) square

Paper punches, ¼ inch (6 mm) and ⅛ inch (3 mm)

Commercially prepared metal clay slip

Kiln shelf

Jeweler's soft brass brush

Rotary tumbler with stainless steel shot and liquid burnishing compound

Liver of sulfur

Flat-nose pliers, 2 pairs

Gold vermeil 5 mm oval jump rings 20

Gold vermeil toggle clasp

Instructions

1 Roll out the clay to the thickness of four playing cards. Cut out five squares each 1¼ inch (3.2 cm) in size, and round the corners with the needle tool. (I made a template out of cardstock, but you can also cut the squares and round the corners when dry with the emery boards.) Set the squares on the hot plate to dry to bone dry.

2 Draw a pencil design onto each square (don't worry, the pencil lines will burn away when the piece is fired). Use your favorite carving tools to carve out the design.

3 Knead the gold clay before opening the package. Keep it warm as you work. Cut very small pieces with the tissue blade and smash the gold into the V-grooves using the blender tool. The firmer the tip the better. Push the clay across the carved line, not with it. Smear away the extra gold clay with the side of the blender tool. Don't be concerned if the surface looks bad at this point. Do all the panels in this way.

4 Set the clay pieces on the hot plate to dry to bone dry. The gold will be the color of yellow ochre when dry. Sand the surface with the ultra-fine sponge sanding pad, or fine-grit emery board. You may need to add more gold after sanding because you may see low spots you've missed. Repeat step 3 and this step until the piece is completely level.

5 Make your own connecting elements with laminated sheet clay (see the sidebar on page 112). They will look like donuts and work to connect each panel of the bracelet with jump rings. Use the small paper punch and punch 20 holes in the four-layer laminate clay sheets. Leave space around the holes as you punch, because the holes you just made will become the centers of the connectors (donuts). Then, using the larger paper punch, try to center it over the holes and "re-punch" them. (This is hard to do, and it's OK if they're not perfectly centered.) Use commercially prepared metal clay slip to attach four connectors on the back of each square, positioned ⅜ inch (9.5 mm) from the side edges (see photo 1, next page) Use the blender tool to wipe away the extra slip.

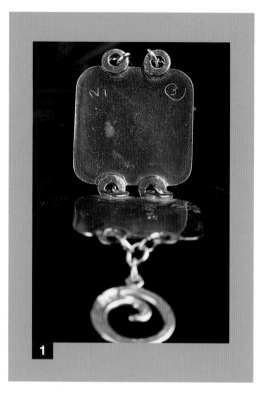

6 When all five panels have four connectors each, it's time to fire. Lay the pieces facedown on a kiln shelf and fire at 1290°F (700°C) for 10 minutes.

7 Use the soft wire brush with soap and water to burnish the surface. Only the soft wire brush should be used on the gold, other brushes could scratch the gold. Tumble for 45 minutes in a rotary tumbler with stainless steel shot and a fresh solution of burnishing compound. Dip in liver of sulfur using the steel tweezers (see page 50). The patina will show a contrast between the polished metals.

8 Use two sets of flat-nose pliers to attach the components of the bracelet: the gold vermeil oval jump rings, and the toggle clasp.

Sheet Clay Lamination

Place a nonstick flexible work surface (baking sheet or ironing pad) on a perfectly flat surface, such as your kitchen counter. Place a sheet of metal clay on top of the work surface and spray a fine mist of water evenly across the surface of the clay. Place another clay sheet on top of the first, being careful not to trap air bubbles (I use a rolling motion as I position the top piece). Next, place another piece of nonstick flexible work surface on top, and weight it down. I use a steel bench block as a weight, but since you are in the kitchen, a cast-iron skillet would work just as well. Let it sit like this for 2 hours and then test at a corner to see if it's dry and ready to come apart. If it's dry, the sheet clay will easily peel away from the work surface. If it's still wet, wait and test the corner again after an hour. This is a two-layer lamination. To make a four-layer lamination, repeat to make two of the two-layer laminated pieces, then laminate them together.

Stacked Ring Set

Create a set of stackable rings in motifs that match any style. Cutting the rings from a single metal clay tube is an easy way to keep the set a consistent size. It's also a fun and convenient way to work.

Stacked Ring Set

Tools & Materials

Metal clay tool kit, (see page 66)

Metric ruler

Calculator

Wax paper

Metal clay rolling pin, or small PVC pipe

Glue stick

Next Generation metal clay, 25 grams

Blender tool, size No. 6

Coffee mug

Hot plate

Next Generation syringe metal clay

Fine and micro-fine sponge sanding pads

Set of calipers

Jeweler's saw frame with 0/6-size saw blades

Vise

Alumina hydrate powder

Kiln shelf

Dust-approved respirator

Jeweler's soft brass brush

Rotary tumbler with mixed stainless steel shot and diluted liquid burnishing compound

Instructions

1 Determine the ring size you want to make and calculate for the metal clay shrinkage when it's fired. Use the guide on page 140 as a worksheet for making these calculations.

2 Next, make a mandrel to fit the ring length, calculated in step 1. Cut a strip of wax paper 2 inches (5 cm) wide, and wrap it around the end of a smaller cylinder, such as a small piece of PVC pipe. Continue adding strips of wax paper until it matches the measurement from step 1. Use the glue stick to secure the end.

3 Roll out a rectangular shape of Next Generation metal clay to the thickness of four playing cards. Wrap the metal clay around the mandrel, and overlap at the seam. Use the tissue blade to cut through both layers of clay at the seam to make a clean butt joint, and remove the extra clay. Stitch together the seam with the blender tool. Set the rolling pin in a coffee mug, metal clay end out, and allow to air dry to the leather hard stage. The ring will slip off the wax paper coil by pulling away from the center. Place the long tube of metal clay on the hot plate to dry.

4 Reinforce the seam on the inside and outside with syringe. Refine the edge with the blender tool. Set the tube on the hot plate to dry. You may notice a lot of little cracks on the edges of the tube. This is typical with this clay formula. When the piece is bone dry you can file the edges with the coarse emery board until the cracks are gone. Use the fine—and then the micro-fine—sponge sanding pads to further refine the ends of the metal clay tube. Use calipers to measure your progress as you sand to ensure that you're keeping the ends of the tube parallel to each other.

5 File the seams with the fine emery board until the seams disappear. Use a wet wipe to further refine the seams, and then rub the entire surface of the metal clay tubing for a smooth finish.

6 Use the calipers to measure one 2 mm band, and cut away this band from the metal clay tube with the jeweler's saw frame using 06 size saw blades. It's helpful to rest the tube on top of a ¾-inch (1.9 cm) opening between the vise jaws. By having the jaws open, it will support the fragile tubing at two points and keep it from rolling. Repeat

this process to cut away; two 3-mm bands, one 4-mm band, and one 5-mm band. Sand the edges of the bands on the micro-fine sponge sanding pad in a figure-eight motion. Turn the ring a quarter of a turn, and sand some more. Repeat this for two more quarter turns.

7 Decorate each band to your liking. Etch a design with a needle tool, or experiment with cutting small circles from gold or silver metal clay and adding them to the side of a ring. I rolled out small, BB-sized balls and attached them to a broad ring using commercially prepared slip as glue.

8 When you're happy with your rings, place all five bone-dry rings in a $\frac{1}{16}$-inch (1.6 mm) layer of alumina hydrate dusted on a kiln shelf and fire at 1650°F (900°C) for 2 hours. The long firing schedule will give the rings optimal strength. Be certain to wear a dust-approved respirator when handling the alumina hydrate, and wash your hands immediately afterward.

9 Finish the rings by burnishing with the soft wire brush with soap and water. Continue to achieve a high polish by using a rotary tumbler with mixed stainless steel shot and a diluted solution of liquid burnishing compound.

Forged Link Necklace

In this striking necklace, the links are actually hammered before firing. The high proportion of binder in First Generation clay holds together even under repeated blows by a planishing hammer.

Tools & Materials

Metal clay tool kit,
  (see page 66)

Cardstock template

First Generation metal clay,
  45 grams

Pair of craft sticks

Hot plate

Steel bench block

Planishing hammer

Rubber bench cube

Kiln shelf

Rotary tumbler with stainless
  steel shot and a diluted
  liquid burnishing com-
  pound

14 sterling silver jump rings,
  16-gauge, 4.4 mm

Flat-nose jeweler's pliers,
  2 pair

Instructions

1 Trace the drawing in figure 1 to make a template out of card stock that's 2⅝ inches (6.6 cm) long.

Figure 1

2 Use your hands to roll out the metal clay into a log shape ¼ inch (6 mm) in diameter and 1 inch (2.5 cm) long. Place the log on the work surface and roll the clay to the thickness of the craft sticks. Place the template on top of the clay and cut out the shape using the pin tool. A dab of olive oil balm on the backside of the template will hold it in place as you trace out the long link shape. Repeat until you have 14 links, and set them on the hot plate to dry to bone dry.

3 Use tweezers to take the links off the hot plate. Set them directly on a steel bench block. The steel will "suck" the heat from the pieces so they'll cool down faster. Strike each link 10 to 20 times using a planishing hammer while the pieces rest on the bench block. The slight dome of the hammer face will give a classic hand-hammered (planished) surface. You'll need to practice the strength of your hammer blows. Don't be surprised if the metal clay starts to crack if you hit it too hard or too many times. I suggest you sacrifice two or three links to learn this technique. Don't hammer too close to the edges because they'll tend to crack.

Forged Link Necklace

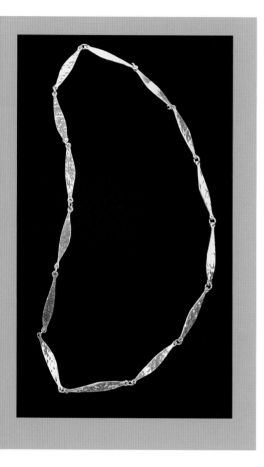

4 Drill the holes using the craft knife like a drill, and carve a ⅛-inch (3 mm) hole on both ends. Be careful not to break the narrow end in this step. I drill on a rubber bench cube (available from metal clay tool suppliers) so there is support under the metal clay as I put pressure on the end. When you have 14 links with no cracks or breaks, arrange them on a kiln shelf (close, but not touching) and fire for 2 hours at 1650°F (900°C).

5 When the pieces are cooled, they're ready to be polished. Wire brush the pieces with soap and water, then place them in a rotary tumbler with stainless steel shot and a diluted liquid burnishing compound. Tumble for 45 minutes. The links will have a dazzling high polish.

6 Join the links with the jump rings. Use two pairs of flat-nose jeweler's pliers to twist open and close the jump rings. Try pairing this necklace with the pendant found on page 88, Cherry Blossoms in Spring (see figure 2), for a beautiful alternative.

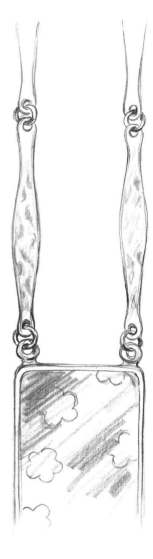

Figure 2

Simple and Elegant Linked Bracelet

The technique of seamlessly building bracelet links illustrates the amazing artistic flexibility of metal clay.

Simple and Elegant Linked Bracelet

Tools & Materials

Metal clay tool kit,
(see page 66)

Next Generation metal clay,
28 grams

Craft sticks

Circular cutters: 7/16-,1/2-,5/8-, 3/4-
inch (1.1 cm, 1.3 cm,
1.6 cm, 1.9 cm) diameters

Hot plate

Metal jeweler's tweezers

Half-round needle file

Paper and a mechanical
pencil with 0.5 lead

Commercially prepared slip

Syringe metal clay

Kiln shelf

Terra-cotta saucer

Alumina hydrate

Rotary tumbler with mixed
stainless steel shot
and liquid burnishing
compound

Instructions

1 Roll out Next Generation metal clay on top of a flexible work surface to the thickness of the craft sticks. Cut out the three different size links (they'll end up looking like donuts) to build the bracelet. For the large links, cut seven circles with the 3/4-inch (1.9 cm) cutter, then cut out the center of these with the 1/2-inch (1.3 cm) cutter. For the medium links, cut out seven links with the 1/2-inch (1.3 cm) cutter, then cut out the centers with the 5/8-inch (1.6 cm) cutter. For the small links (used to make the chain to the clasp), you'll need to cut out three links using the 5/8-inch (1.6 cm) cutter, then cut out the centers of these with the 7/16-inch (1.1 cm) cutter.

2 Gently pick up each donut-shaped link with your fingers, and stretch them (by pulling) into an oval. Repeat this for all 17 links. Set them on a hot plate, and allow to dry.

3 Remove the oval-shaped links from the hot plate using tweezers and set them on the flexible work surface. When the links have cooled to the touch, file the inside using a half-round needle file to refine the edges. File the outside of each link with the fine emery board.

4 Select one of the largest links to be the first link of the bracelet—this will be part of the clasp. To make the clasp, trace the inside of this link on a piece of paper using the mechanical pencil. Carefully cut out this paper pattern. Roll out a marble-size piece of Next Generation metal clay to the thickness of craft sticks. Use your finger to brush some olive oil hand balm onto the surface of the paper. Place the olive oil side down on the rolled out clay. The olive oil will keep the pattern in place. Cut out the oval shape by using a pin tool. Set on the hot plate to dry thoroughly.

5 Arrange the large and medium links in a pattern you find pleasing. Cut every other link in half using a sharp, clean tissue blade. Starting with the second link, use a blending tool to load a good-size dollop of commercially prepared slip on each of the cut ends. Slide on link number one and number three, then glue the number two link back together. Press together tightly and hold to the count of 10, then set on the hot plate to dry. The slip will dry quickly. You now have three links that are linked together. Repeat this process to create the next three links of the chain. Link these two sets of three and three together.

You now have seven links completed. Congratulations, you're halfway there! Repeat the process you used to create the first seven links. This should give you 14 large and medium links. Link together the three small links, then attach this strand to end of the chain.

6 To complete the clasp (see detail, right), take the last small link and file a flat edge with the coarse emery board. Attach the oval disk you made in step 4 to the flattened edge of the last small link using the syringe like glue. Wipe away the extra syringe clay with the blender tool and set the entire bracelet on the hot plate to dry.

7 When all the components of the chain are completely dry, file all the links, inside and outside, and eliminate any extra syringe clay that's sticking out. To file the inside, use the half-round needle file. For the outside, the fine emery board will work best. Rub the outside of each link with a wet wipe to get a smooth surface. Let it dry overnight before firing.

8 Place the bracelet on a kiln shelf a terra-cotta flower saucer filled halfway with alumina hydrate. Set the bracelet in the alumina and wiggle it to get alumina between each of the links. Bury the bracelet completely by filling the saucer with alumina hydrate. Fire in a kiln set to 1650°F (900°C) for 2 hours. This firing schedule will give the pieces maximum strength.

9 After firing, let everything cool to room temperature and take the bracelet out of the alumina hydrate. If any of the links have fused together, hold the bracelet by the clasp end and aggressively slap the bracelet on a hard surface. This will break the fused links apart. If this doesn't work, the fused links can be carefully sawn apart with a jeweler's saw.

10 Finish the piece by tumbling with stainless steel shot and burnishing solution for 45 minutes to an hour.

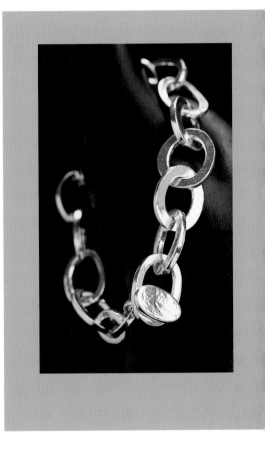

Gold and Cubic Zirconia Ring

Recognize all the special gifts someone brings into your life with this one-of-kind ring made of 22-karat gold metal clay and tiny cubic zirconia stones.

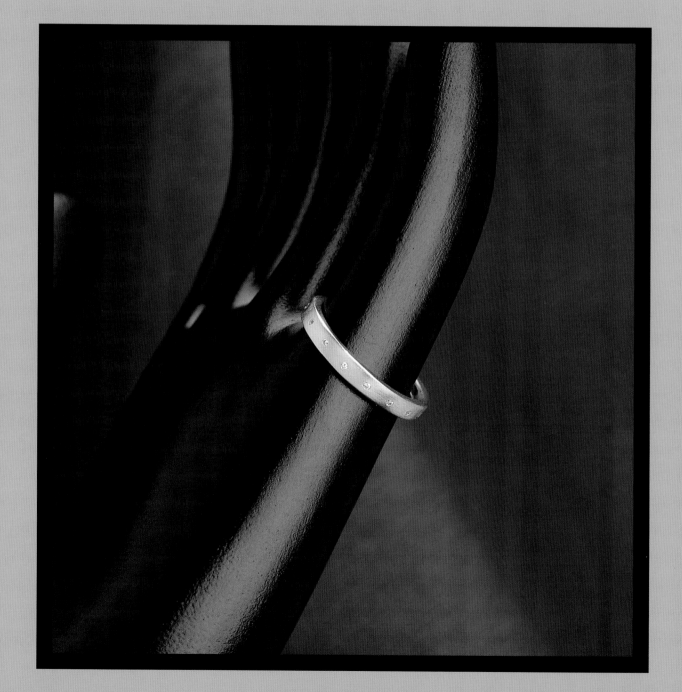

Metal clay tool kit,
(see page 66)

Metric ruler

Newspaper

Glue stick

22-karat gold metal clay

Hot plate

Metal cutting drill bit, 1 mm

14 cubic zirconia stones, 1 mm

Clear plastic ruler

Kiln shelf

Alumina hydrate

Respirator with approved dust
cartridges

Jeweler's soft wire brush

Instructions

1 Determine the size of the ring you wish to make, then calculate for the shrinkage of the material as it's fired. There's a helpful chart on page 140 (for eight playing cards in thickness) that will quickly walk you through the steps.

2 Next, make a newspaper mandrel to fit your ring length (from step 1). Cut a long, 1-inch-wide (2.5 cm) strip of newspaper, and wrap it around the handle end of the needle tool. Continue adding to the strip of newspaper until it matches the paper pattern from your calculations in step 1. Use the glue stick to secure the end of the newspaper.

3 Roll out a snake of gold metal clay at least half as long as the paper pattern. Roll the snake flat to the thickness of eight playing cards (about 2 mm). Wrap the gold clay around the newspaper mandrel, and overlap at the seam. Using the tissue blade, cut through both layers at an angle, and use the blender tool to close the seam. Set the ring aside to dry to leather hard. The ring will come off the newspaper coil when you pull the tool out from the center. This will not put pressure on the ring, which is very fragile at this stage. Place the ring on a hot plate to dry to bone dry.

4 Fill the ring's inside seam with a thread-size snake of gold clay. Use the blender tool to smooth the seam and set the ring back on the hot plate to dry. Do the same on the front seam, if needed. When the ring is dry, file the edges and the seam with a brand new fine emery board until the edges are smooth and crisp. (This emery board can be sent to a fine metal recycler to reclaim the gold dust.)

5 To set the tiny cubic zirconia stones, drill into the band with a 1 mm drill bit. Dip the end of the pin tool in olive oil balm, and touch the top of one of the stones. The balm will stick to the stone so you can lift it. Set the stone into the drilled hole. Repeat for all 13 remaining stones. Using the plastic ruler, press firmly on top of the stones to set them level with the surface of the ring band. The shrinkage will take care of holding the stones in place.

6 Place the ring on its side on a kiln shelf sprinkled with a light dusting of alumina hydrate. Safety note: Be certain to wear a dust-approved respirator when handling alumina hydrate and wash your hands immediately. Fire the ring at 1650°F (900°C) for at least 10 minutes. I fired my ring for 2 hours for optimal strength, and knowing that the stones can handle this firing schedule. Use a soft wire brush with soapy water to finish the ring.

Silver Twig Pin

The play of light off the silver and cubic zirconia stones of this piece reflects its wintry inspiration. Metal clay slip is a perfect medium for turning common things into brilliant works of art.

Tools & Materials

Metal clay tool kit, (see page 66)

Twig, at least 3¼ inches (8.3 cm) long

Commercially prepared slip

Distilled water

Eye dropper

Hot plate

Brass tubing: 8 mm, 7 mm, 6 mm, 5.5 mm, and 5 mm

Sliding gauge or gauge caliper

Flexible shaft or rotary tool

Stone-setting burs, sizes: 6 mm, 5 mm, 4 mm, 3.5 mm, and 3 mm

Cubic zirconia stones: 6 mm, 5 mm, 4 mm, 3.5 mm, and 3 mm, 1 each

Syringe metal clay

Sterling silver pin joint and catch

Terra-cotta saucer filled with vermiculite

Soft brass wire brush

Nickel silver pin stem

Needle-nose and flat-nose pliers

Instructions

1 Select a twig with lots of branches in a relatively short distance. For example, the twig used in this project measured only 3¼ inches (8.3 cm) long, and branched off seven times from the main stem. This provided a lot of potential places to set a stone.

2 Add 10 drops of distilled water from an eyedropper to a new jar of commercially prepared slip. Smooth consistency is best; homemade slip is not as smooth for capturing details; trust me, I've tried. Mix the water into the slip with a needle tool. Apply a layer of this thinned slip on the twig with a paintbrush. Set on the hot plate to dry. Repeat to build up 12 layers of slip allowing it to dry between each new coat. Because of evaporation, you will need to add a drop or two of water to the slip and mix well before each coat.

3 For the bur stone setting technique (see page 57), you'll need a piece of brass tubing slightly larger than the stone.

Stone and Bur Size	Brass Tubing Size	Minimal Plug Depth
6 mm	8 mm	4 mm
5 mm	7 mm	4 mm
4 mm	6 mm	3 mm
3.5 mm	5.5 mm	3 mm
3 mm	5 mm	3 mm

Cut out five plugs from Next Generation metal clay with brass tubing (see the size chart above). With the clay still inside, set the brass tubing on the hot plate to dry. As the clay dries, it shrinks slightly. It becomes easier to remove by pushing it out with a smaller diameter piece of brass tubing. File the dry plugs with the fine-grit emery board until the top and bottom are level. Use a sliding gauge or gauge caliper to make sure the plug is at least 1 mm deeper than the height of the stone.

4 Cut the center of the plugs with the craft knife by using a drilling motion and cut a small hole all the way through. Use the flex shaft and a stone setting bur to cut out a seat for the stone. Check the depth by placing the stone in the hole you cut. The stone needs to sit ⅛ inch

Silver Twig Pin

(3 mm) below the rim of the plug for a tension fit (allowing for the 10 to 15 percent shrinkage for this type of clay).

5 When you have a perfect fit for all the stones, glue the settings in place with the syringe clay. Use the blender tool to wipe away any extra material that oozes out. On the back of the setting, add extra syringe clay to make a strong connection. Set the piece on the hot plate to dry thoroughly. Set the stones and check to see that they're level. Use the eyedropper to place a drop of clean water on the top of the stone and place back on the hot plate. The water activates the binder in the clay body and will tack the stone in place, holding it until the bezel shrinks in firing. Attach the joint and catch pieces on the back of the twig by using syringe to glue the pieces in place.

6 Fire in a terra-cotta saucer filled with vermiculite for at least 10 minutes at 1650°F (900°C). It's typical to get some cracks in the pieces using this technique. Repair the cracks by piping syringe in the same direction of the crack. Use the No. 0 blender tool to push the clay into the cracks by going across the open crack. Use the side of the blender tool to wipe away the extra clay on the surface. Brush a thin layer of slip over the repair because it will mimic the rest of the texture, and the repair will disappear. Fire again in vermiculite for 2 hours at 1650°F (900°C). I fire for 2 hours at 1650°F (900°C) every time I add new material to metal clay that has already been fired.

7 For the surface finish, use the soft wire brush with soap and water to gently brush the brooch. Don't worry—wire brushing won't harm the stones. Set the pin stem with needle-nose and flat-nose pliers (see photo 1). I always use a nickel silver pin stem because it is sturdier than sterling silver and doesn't need to be work hardened before setting. Nickel is a strong metal alloy and can go through denim without bending.

1

Patience in a Square

The art of origami has a rich tradition meant to teach patience and discipline, leading the artist toward balance and perfection. In these two pins, the paper-like characteristics of sheet metal clay led to stunning results.

Patience in a Square

Tools & Materials

Metal clay tool kit,
(see page 66)

Sheet metal clay, square
product, 2 pieces

Paper punch, ⅛ inch (3 mm)

Cubic zirconia, 4 mm

Hard solder, paste flux,
torch, or two-part epoxy

Sterling silver catch and join,
or ¾-inch (1.9 cm) glue-on
steel pin back

Thermal ceramic firing wool

Soft bristle brass brush

Nickel silver pin stem

Super-flush cutters

Jeweler's flat needle file

Needle-nose pliers

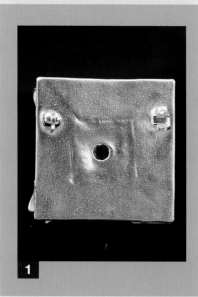

Instructions

1 Fold a square sheet of metal clay following the diagrams for folding in figures 1 through 8 at the bottom of the next page. In figure 8, you can fold down or curl back the folded points that will extend from the corners.

2 Cut a ¼-inch (6 mm) square piece of sheet clay. Using a craft knife, cut an X in the center of the square, but don't go too close to the edge. Stop cutting when you get within ¹⁄₁₆-inch (1.6 mm) of each corner (see page 60 for more on this stone-setting technique).

3 Lift the center folds of the origami piece, and using the paper punch, punch a hole in the center. Place the inverted stone (upside down) on top of the center punch. Lay the square piece (with the X cut) centered on top of the stone. The stone will peek through the cut. Carefully brush water around the outside edge of the square piece of clay sheet holding the stone. This may be tricky, because you have to fold back the center flaps of the folded origami piece one at a time and then brush the water.

4 When I created these pieces, I sealed all the folds with a slightly damp watercolor brush. To do this, dip the watercolor brush in water, wipe off most of the water on the back of your hand, then dampen a seam and press the fold down with your finger. Sealing all the folds this way will make a stronger piece of jewelry.

5 Punch out two holes from a sheet of metal clay with the hole punch. Take the two disks you punched out and brush them with a little water. Attach them onto the back where the components of the pin back—the catch, and joint—will be soldered after firing (see photo 1).

6 Fire the piece with the stone side (front side) up on a kiln shelf at 1650°F (900°C) for 10 minutes.

7 Use the burnishing tool to burnish the paper clay dots that were added to the back of the piece in step 5. Use hard solder, paste flux, and a torch to attach the catch and joint. As soon as the solder has flowed, use steel tweezers to lift the piece and immediately set between two pieces of ceramic firing wool. Keep the piece between the wool for 15 to 30 minutes and don't peek. **NOTE:** Setting the piece between the firing wool allows the piece (most importantly the stone) to cool slowly. Fast cooling would cause too great of a temperature shock and the stone may crack. Thermal ceramic firing wool is available from lampworking glass suppliers or some metal clay suppliers. If you can't solder, it's a great time to learn. For another option, use a two-part epoxy to attach a ¾-inch (1.9 cm) steel pin back.

8 Finish by brushing the piece with the soft brass wire brush. Cut the pin stem with super-flush cutters to fit, and file to a point with a jeweler's flat needle file. Burnish the tip of the pin stem by hand to smooth out the file marks. Set the pin in place and close the joint with flat-nose needle-nose pliers.

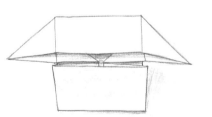

Figure 1

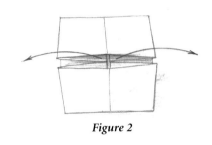

Figure 2

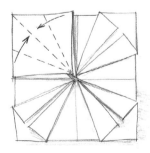

Figure 3

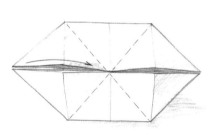

Figure 4

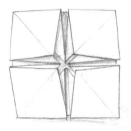

Figure 5

Figure 6

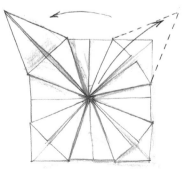

Figure 7

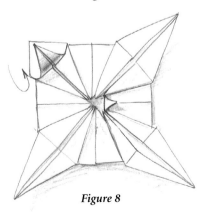

Figure 8

Lunar Phase Ring

A recent innovation in metal clay allows the artist to use fire-in-place stones, such as this brilliantly luminous moonstone. To complete the lunar theme, decorations around the ring show the moon in its various phases.

Tools & Materials

Metal clay tool kit, (see page 66)

4 craft sticks

Wood glue

Binder clips

Next Generation metal clay

Brass plunger-style cutter, ¾-inch (1.9 cm) diameter

Hot plate

Moonstone cabochon, 14 mm

Half-round needle file

Kiln shelf

Second Generation metal clay

Sheet metal clay (4 layers, laminated)

Paper punch, ¼ inch

Ring mandrel

Rawhide mallet

Next Generation metal clay syringe

Vermiculite

Jeweler's soft wire brush

Instructions

1 First, you'll need to make extra-thick spacers. Glue two craft sticks together with a thin layer of wood glue. Clamp them with the binder clip until the glue dries. Repeat for the other two craft sticks. Roll out a marble-size ball of Next Generation clay to the thickness of the double-stacked craft sticks. Use a ¾-inch (1.9 cm) diameter brass plunger-style cutter to cut a plug from the moist clay. Set the cutter (with the metal clay still inside) on the hot plate to dry.

2 When the clay is bone dry, plunge it out of the brass cutter, and carve out the center with a craft knife. Start carving by using the craft knife like a drill to cut a hole in the center of the plug of clay. Continue carving away material from the inside until the stone fits in the bezel. Use a half-round needle file to remove some more material so the stone has a loose fit. Taking away this extra material will compensate for the shrinkage. If the fit is too tight, the force of the shrinkage could crack the stone when fired. Fire the stone in the bezel set on a kiln shelf at 1110°F (600°C) for 45 minutes.

3 To make the band, roll out a snake of Second Generation metal clay to the thickness of five playing cards. Use the chart (on the next page) to determine how long to make the ring band. Trim the edges with the tissue blade to 7/16 inch (1.1 cm) wide. Set on the hot plate to dry.

4 Make a four-layer sheet of laminated sheet clay (see page 112 for more on making four-layer laminated sheet clay). When the band is bone dry, remove it from the hot plate. Punch out small circles from the laminated sheet clay with the paper punch. Alter these discs with the paper punch to resemble different phases in the lunar cycle. Decorate the band with moon shapes by attaching them with a light brush of water. Set on the hot plate to dry. File a beveled edge on the back side of the band with the fine emery board.

5 Lay the strip flat on a kiln shelf, and fire for 2 hours at 1650°F (900°C). Remember, the longer firing time will yield the strongest and densest metal from this formula of metal clay.

Lunar Phase Ring

Ring Sizing Chart
Double-Fired Ring made with Next Generation Metal Clay

Size	Length in mm
4	56
4.5	58
5	59
5.5	61
6	62
6.5	64
7	65
7.5	67
8	68
8.5	70
9	71
9.5	73
10	74
10.5	75
11	76
11.5	77
12	79
12.5	80
13	81
13.5	82

6 Bend the ring band with your fingers around a ring mandrel. It's possible to bend fine silver with your fingers, and it's better than using pliers because pliers can leave a mark on the soft silver. With the ring on the mandrel, use the rawhide mallet to refine the shape. Place the bezel-set stone between the gap of the ring band. It may take some patience to get a perfect fit. Fill the join with syringe clay by pushing the soft material into the gap with the blender tool. Set the ring on the hot plate to dry.

7 Place the ring in a pile of vermiculite heaped on a kiln shelf with the stone facedown. Fire at 1650°F (900°C) for 30 minutes. This temperature didn't affect my moonstone. If you'd like to use a different natural stone, I recommend you run a test firing of the stone alone in the kiln at 1650°F (900°C) for 30 minutes to see if it can survive this firing schedule.

8 Use the soft wire brush with soap and water to give a soft satin finish to the ring. The soft wire brush will not harm the moonstone.

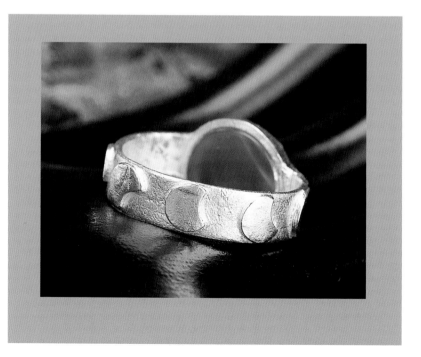

Garnet and Silver Necklace

Next Generation metal clay has a lower firing temperature than its First Generation counterpart. This difference opens the door for some stunning design options, such as the fire-in-place stones found on this necklace.

Garnet and Silver Necklace

Tools & Materials

Metal clay tool kit,
    (see page 66)

Next Generation metal clay,
    32 grams

Pair of craft sticks

Circle cutter, 7mm

Rotary tool with drill bit, $\frac{1}{32}$-inch
    (0.8 mm)

Hot plate

Kiln shelf

22-gauge brass wire

Rotary tumbler with mixed
    stainless steel shot and
    liquid burnishing compound

3 almandine garnet cabochons,
    4 mm round

3 bamboo skewers

Fabric glue

Foam block

Commercially prepared slip

Syringe metal clay

Circle cutter or plastic
    beverage straw with 2 mm
    diameter

Circle cutters, ⅜ inch (9.5 mm)
    and ¾ inch (1.9 cm)

Jeweler's half-round needle file

Vermiculite

16-inch strand of garnet
    faceted button beads, 5 mm

Bead wire, 21 strand, stainless
    steel and nylon coated

4 sterling silver crimp beads

Flat-nose pliers

Super-flush cutters

Instructions

1 To make the spacer beads, roll out the Next Generation metal clay to the thickness of craft sticks. Cut as many circles as you can with a 7 mm cutter. (I was able to cut 25 circles in the first roll. I balled up and rolled out the remaining clay and was able to cut out 11 more. All this from a 25 gram package). While the clay is still moist, poke a hole directly in the center of each circle with the needle tool. Set these circles on the hot plate to dry. When the circles are bone dry, make a hole in the center with the drill bit and flexible shaft. Make a total of 59 of these spacer beads.

2 To finish the edges, thread one bead at a time onto the end of the needle tool. Use a wet wipe to smooth the edges as you spin the bead on the needle tool. Remove the bead from the needle tool and set on the hot plate for about 1 minute to drive off the moisture. Repeat for the remaining 58 spacer beads.

3 Line all the spacer beads flat on a kiln shelf. Fire at 1290°F (700°C) for at least 10 minutes.

4 When cool, thread the spacer beads onto the 22-gauge brass wire. (After tumbling, it will be much easier to retrieve the spacer beads strung on the wire.) Twist the wire to make a closed loop. Tumble the strand for 1 hour in a rotary tumbler with stainless steel shot and a diluted liquid burnishing compound.

5 To make the bar clasp, glue the top (the domed end) of one of the 4-mm almandine garnet cabochons to the blunt end of a bamboo skewer using a drop of fabric glue (see figure 1). Repeat for the other two stones. Poke the sharp end of the skewer in a block of foam and allow the glue to dry.

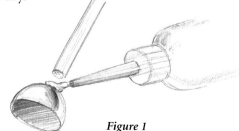

Figure 1

6 Remove the skewer from the foam. Dip the stone into commercially prepared slip, covering at least two-thirds of the stone (see figure 2). Use a twisting motion as you dip down, and keep twisting as you remove. Place the skewer back into the foam block and allow the slip to dry around the stone. Repeat this process, building two to three layers of slip. This will become the bezel for the stone. Repeat the process for the other two cabochons.

7 Remove the stone from the skewer by peeling the glue off the stone. Gently file the back of the slip-covered stone with the fine-grit emery board until you get a 2 mm-wide flat surface. Roll out a coil of Next Generation metal clay ¾ inch (1.9 cm) long and ⅛ inch (3 mm) in diameter. Let it dry to bone dry on the hot plate. File the ends of the coil with the coarse emery board. Use syringe clay to attach the stones to each end. Wipe away any extra syringe with a small blender tool. Set the piece on the hot plate to dry.

8 Roll out a slab of Next Generation metal clay to the thickness of a craft stick. Use a cutter to cut out a 7-mm-wide circle. Use a 2-mm circle cutter (or plastic beverage straw) to cut out a hole directly in the center of the 7-mm circle. Make two of these donut-shaped pieces and set them on the hot plate to dry to bone dry. Remove one from the hot plate, and flatten one spot on the edge of the circle by filing it with the coarse emery board. Repeat for the other piece and set aside. Glue one edge of the donut-shaped piece to the center of the bar using metal clay syringe (keep the second piece for use later in step 10). Use the blender tool to wipe away any excess.

9 To make the toggle, roll out a marble-sized ball of Next Generation metal clay to craft stick thickness. Cut out a ¾-inch (1.9 cm) circle with a cutter. Cut out a ⅜-inch (9.5 mm) circle from the center. Set this piece on the hot plate to dry to bone dry. While this piece is drying, roll out a coil of silver clay 1 inch (2.5 cm) long, and 2 mm in diameter. Take the donut piece from the hot plate and attach the moist coil of clay centered on the donut with a brush of water (see figure 3). Use the blender tool to blend the seam, then set the circle back on the hot plate until the

Figure 2

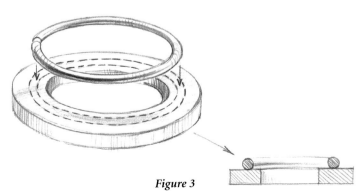

Figure 3

Garnet and Silver Necklace

1

newly added coil of clay is dry. (You don't have to make the seam perfect because most of it will be cut away when it's dry.) With the craft knife, cut away just enough of the dry clay at the seam to hold the third stone. Go slowly, and check the stone's fit as you go. Take your time to achieve good craftsmanship. When you get a perfect fit, glue the stone setting in place using syringe clay. Wipe away the extra syringe clay with a blender tool. Let the syringe dry by putting the piece back on the hot plate for 1 minute.

10 Attach the little circle from step 8 onto the edge of the donut, just behind the stone setting, by using a small amount of syringe (see photo 1). Wipe away any excess with the blender tool. Set the toggle on the hot plate for 1 minute. After it's dry, sand the outside edges with the coarse emery board, then use the fine emery board to smooth the outside edge. To get an ultra-smooth surface, use a wet wipe on the edges. To refine the inside edges of the donut, use a craft knife to carve away any imperfections, then use a jeweler's half-round needle file and smooth with a wet wipe.

11 Set the toggle on a kiln shelf. Place the bar clasp in a small pile of vermiculite on the same kiln shelf, and fire these pieces at 1110°F (600°C) for 30 minutes. This is the lowest firing temperature possible for including natural stones. See page 53 for a complete list of natural stones tested in metal clay at this firing schedule.

12 To polish the toggle and bar clasp, tumble the pieces for 1 hour in a rotary tumbler with stainless steel shot and a diluted burnishing compound. Surprisingly, tumbling will not damage the stones.

13 Complete the necklace by stringing all the garnet beads and the silver clay spacer beads together in a random pattern on a beading wire. Attach the toggle on one end with two sterling silver crimp beads by using flat-nose pliers to close the crimp beads. Attach the bar clasp at the other end in the same way. Trim the extra wire with super-flush wire cutters.

Kum Boo Fan Brooch

Create this exquisite brooch using an ancient Korean metalsmithing technique for combining silver and gold called kum boo. The result is intense beauty.

Kum Boo Fan Brooch

Tools & Materials

Metal clay tool kit, (see page 66)

Second Generation metal clay, 24 grams

Cardstock

Kanji texture rubber stamp

Stencil brush

Chinese coin or similar

Hot plate

Jeweler's square needle file

Syringe metal clay

Kiln shelf

24-karat gold foil

Tissue paper

Cuticle scissors

Portable electric burner and ¼ inch (6 mm) steel block, or trinket kiln with brass insert

Bamboo skewers

Leather work gloves

Long-handled steel tweezers, 10 inches (2.4 cm) or longer

Metal or agate burnisher

Round and flat needle-nose pliers

Nickel one-piece narrow pin back, hard silver solder, paste flux, and nickel pickle, or glue-on pin back and industrial strength two-part epoxy

Soft wire brush for gold

Flexible shaft tool with brass wire brush attachment

Drill bit, ⅛ inch (3 mm)

Liver of sulfur

Assorted decorative beads

20-gauge sterling silver wire

Instructions

1 Make a fan-shaped template from the cardstock that measures 3 x 1½ inches (7.6 x 3.8 cm). Roll out half of an 18-gram package of Second Generation metal clay to the thickness of three playing cards. Press a rubber stamp across the surface of the moist clay. Place the template on the surface and cut the shape out with the pin tool.

2 For the backing piece, roll out more clay and lay the template on its surface. Use the thin tissue blade and flex it to fit the shape. Cut the clay ⅜ inch (9.5 mm) larger than the template. Texture the surface using a stencil brush in a stippling motion.

3 For the third layer, roll out some more clay to the thickness of two playing cards. Press a Chinese coin (or something similar) into the surface.

4 Set all three layers on a hot plate to dry. When bone dry, refine the edges with the emery boards, moving from coarse to fine. Use a craft knife to carve out the square in the center of the coin's imprint (if applicable). Use a jeweler's square needle file to refine the corners. By drying the pieces first, you can get really sharp and crisp edges.

5 Laminate the pieces together by using syringe metal clay like glue between each layer. Use the blender tool to wipe away extra syringe. File a 45° beveled angle on the outside edge of this laminated piece with the fine emery file.

6 Place the laminated piece flat on a kiln shelf and fire for 10 minutes at 1650°F (900°C). Don't touch the piece with your fingers after it comes out of the kiln. For the kum boo technique, you don't want the oils and dirt from your fingers to contaminate the surface. Oils will act as a "resist" (meaning, the gold won't bond any place you've touched). Use tweezers to remove the piece from the kiln shelf.

7 Sandwich the 24-karat gold foil between tissue paper, and cut the foil with cuticle scissors. Use the craft knife to cut out the square in the center of the circle.

8 Set a ¼-inch (6 mm) steel block on a portable electric burner, like the stovetop version. Set the heat to high and wait for the steel to warm up. Use tweezers to place the fired metal clay piece, fresh from the kiln, on top of the steel plate. Wait about 10 minutes for the metal clay piece to heat up.

9 Position the gold exactly where you want it (using tweezers). While wearing the leather gloves, use the long tweezers to hold the piece and use the burnisher to tack down the gold. You will know it's ready if the gold "sticks" to the metal clay as a result of the tacking motion.

10 Next, start rubbing the gold foil with the burnishing tool in a circular motion. If the gold is not burnishing to a high gloss, stop and wait because it's not heated to the correct temperature. Continue burnishing until the gold is nice and shiny. The 24-karat gold looks fabulous when hand-burnished. The next time you kum boo, try using a lower gold karat foil, or combine the different karat types on one piece.

11 Using needle-nose pliers, take the pin stem out of the one-piece pin back. Solder the pin back onto the back, positioned at the top third of the piece (see photo 1), so it hangs properly when it's worn and doesn't flop over. Allow everything to air cool, then place in a solution of nickel pickle. An alternative to soldering would be to glue on a one-piece pin back with an industrial strength two-part epoxy.

12 Finish with a soft wire brush and soap and water. Use a brass brush attachment on the flex shaft to get the lower area inside the square. You'll need to hand-burnish the gold again at this point unless you prefer the look of the gold with the soft wire brush. This piece could be finished in a variety of ways. Option 1: Use the flex shaft and the ⅛-inch (3 mm) drill bit to drill a hole centered on the bottom edge of the pin as a place to hang decorative beads. Add beads by wire wrapping using 20-gauge sterling silver round wire. Position the pin stem in place, and tighten with the flat-nose pliers (see photo 1). Option 2: Dip the piece in a weak solution of liver of sulfur and play with the patina (see page 50). The liver of sulfur won't patina the gold, so have fun with no worries of changing its appearance.

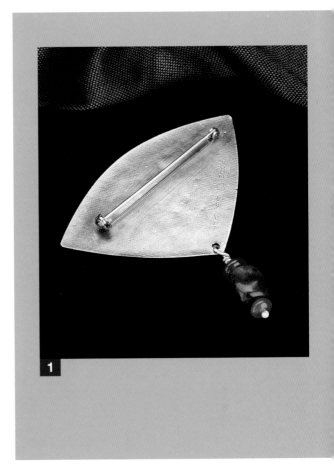

1

Ring-Sizing Guide for Second and Next Generation Metal Clay

For clay that has been rolled to the thickness of four playing cards:

1 Wrap a strip of paper tightly around your knuckle. Mark the exact point exactly where the paper overlaps. Measure this distance using a metric ruler:_____mm.

2 Add 2 mm for the thickness of the band: _____mm + 2 mm = _____mm.

3 Adjust for the shrinkage by multiplying the total by 1.14. If the number after the decimal point is 5 or higher, round up to the next whole number. For example, if your number after multiplying is 70.68 mm, make the ring 71 mm long. Your total from step 2: _____ mm x 1.14 = _____ mm. Mark this new length on the strip of paper. This is how long you will need to make the ring.

For clay that has been rolled to the thickness of eight playing cards:

1 Wrap a strip of paper tightly around your knuckle. Mark the exact point exactly where the paper overlaps. Measure this distance using a metric ruler:_____mm.

2 Add 4 mm for the thickness of the band: _____mm + 4 mm = _____mm.

3 Adjust for the shrinkage by multiplying the total by 1.14. If the number after the decimal point is 5 or higher, round up to the next whole number. For example, if your number after multiplying is 70.68 mm, make the ring 71 mm long. Your total from step 2: _____ mm x 1.14 = _____ mm. Mark this new length on the strip of paper. This is how long you will need to make the ring.

Cuff Style Bracelet Sizing Chart

Second Generation and Next Generation Metal Clay

These measurements allow for 14 percent shrinkage in a bracelet that is 2 mm thick (rolled out with craft stick spacers).

Baby: 11.3 cm
Child (small): 12.3 cm
Child (large): 13.2 cm
Woman (small): 14.5 mm
Woman (medium): 15.5 cm
Woman (large): 16.8 cm
Man (small): 17.2 cm
Man (medium): 18.3 cm
Man (large): 19.5 cm

For a Custom Fit:

1 Wrap a piece of paper around your wrist and tape it in place so you can get an accurate fit. Leave a ⅞-inch (2.2 cm) opening, and mark the paper on both sides of the gap. The opening is so the cuff-style bracelet can slip on and off at the thinnest part of your wrist. Take the paper off and measure its length; insert your measurement here (for example, 14 cm)_____.

2 Add 4 mm to the measurement in step 1. Convert the total to millimeters. Example: 14 cm equals 140 mm. (140 mm + 4 mm = 144 mm). Your measurement _____+ 4 mm =_____. Convert to millimeters =_____.

3 Multiply the total from step 2 by 1.14 (adding 14 percent for the shrinkage). Example: 144 mm x 1.14 = 164.16 mm. Your total from step 2 _____ x 1.14 = _____. Convert back to cm by simply moving the decimal point one space to the left; To continue the example, 164.16 mm = 16.4 cm. The bracelet should be 16.4 cm long.

Glossary of Terms

Abrade: to remove the top layer of the metal by sanding, filing, or grinding.

Air dry: to allow the ambient air to dry clay over time. The time is affected by the presence or lack of humidity.

Bone dry: the state when no moisture or water molecules are present and only binder and pure metal particles remain.

Burnish: to make smooth, bright, or glossy with the use of a tool rubbed across the surface of the metal.

Carcinogen: a material known to cause cancer from either short-term or long-term exposure.

Coefficiency of Expansion, or COE: the measurable difference between a piece of glass when it is hot and when it is cool. Hot glass expands when hot and shrinks when cool. Each formula and color of glass has a different COE.

Concave: to curve or bow inwards, as in a bowl shape.

Convex: to curve or bow outwards, as in a dome shape.

Crash cool: to rapidly cool a piece of glass (dichroic) to 1000°F (538°C) to prevent clouding (devitrification) on the surface.

Dichroic glass: a layered glass that has an opalescent quality.

Extender: a solution of glycerin, water, and food color. It is used by kneading into a lump form of metal clay to slow down evaporation, thus extending the wet working time.

Float glass: the same as windowpane glass.

Glass annealing: to cool to a specific temperature unique for that formula of glass to prevent cracking.

Glass slumping: to shape hot glass using the ever-present force of gravity.

Inclusions: in gemology, any foreign matter, solid or liquid, enclosed in the mass mineral or crystal. In metal clay, inclusions are any object, other than metal clay, that can be fired at the same time.

Inert: to have few or no active properties, neutral.

Kum boo (pronounced Come-Boo): an ancient Korean metals technique in which high karat gold is permanently bonded to fine silver using low heat and pressure.

Malleable: a metal that can be hammered, shaped, or pressed into various shapes and/or returned to its original shape.

Matrix: a mold material used in rubber stamp production.

Media: material like paint, fabric, metal, etc.

Mitered joint: formed by the junction of two ends beveled at equal 45° angles.

Nonferrous metal: copper, brass, sterling silver, fine silver, and all varieties of gold. Literally means that no iron is present.

Opaque: solid color; in enameling and glass work, it is a color that is not transparent.

Patina/patination: a surface oxidation created with the controlled use of a chemical or combination of chemicals.

Pickle: a mild acid used to dissolve residue flux and surface oxides that develop when metal is heated, as in soldering.

Porcelain: a high-fire clay body traditionally fired above 2300°F (1260°C) it is very hard, very white, and translucent where thin.

Powdered metal technology: a process where metal is melted to a liquefied state, then sprayed (atomized) under extreme pressure into a gas-filled chamber. The gas used will affect the size and shape of the metal powder. The size of the metal powder can range in size from 5 to 20 microns, and the shape varies from a compact sphere to a loose flake.

Pyrometer: a device that displays the temperature, and a programmable pyrometer will watch the temperature for you and keep it at a constant rate.

Regulator: a device used to regulate the flow of compressed gas, air, or oxygen.

Release agent: used to help remove clay from a mold.

Simulant gemstones: man-made of any material to mimic the appearance of the natural stone.

Sintering: when the pure metal particles bond in the presence of heat. Unlike fusing, the metal particles do not melt; there is a bond on a microscopic level.

Slab construction: In metal clay, bone dry slabs are simply joined with slip.

Slurry: the same as slip; it is a mixture of clay and water.

Sodium bisulphate: a chemical that, when diluted with water, can be used as pickle. It is commonly sold as a swimming pool chemical for raising the pH level.

Solder: joining two metals by means of an intermediate alloy that melts at a lower temperature.

Synthetic gemstones: man-made of the same chemical composition and crystal structure as the natural stone.

Thermocouple: a probe that sticks out in the kiln chamber. It takes the temperature and acts like a thermometer.

Traditional enameling: uses vitreous glass powder, glass fused metal.

Virgin clay: untouched by human hands.

Water etching: a technique using a resist and water to take away the surface of the clay.

Acknowledgments

Thank you to all the amazing artists who contributed work for the gallery section of this book. Metal clay continues to test our creativity, and your contributions add depth and variety to this book. Keep up the pivotal work!

Thanks to the gang at Lark: Jimmy Knight, Marthe LeVan, Steve Mann, Kathy Holmes, Stewart O'Shields, the whole Lark team, and all the other hard-working souls who made this book possible. A special thanks to Carol Taylor and Rob Pulleyn for having faith in my first project and taking the gamble to do it all again.

My sincere gratitude goes to Tim McCreight for your wisdom, patience, and technical advice. I continue to cherish our working friendship and creative partnership.

Jeanette Landenwitch, Chris Darway, Barbara Becker Simon, Celie Fago, Jennifer Kahn, Babette, Terry Kolvalcik, Chris Ramsay, Maximus Cooper, Chet Bolin, J. Fred Woell, and Tonya Davidson, thank you for being the most inspirational group of artists and friends. Your willingness to share your metal clay discoveries have found their way into the pages of this book. Thank you for being so generous.

Thanks to Andrea Hill, Kevin Whitmore, Diana Montoya, Yvonne Padilla, Gail Philippi, and Virginia Dickson for keeping me employed, "on the road," and teaching.

Phil Hendricks, Maddy Weisz, Hansie Montoya, Nancy Namath, Cole and McKenna O'Donnell, Jo Luttrell, Craig, Cyndy, Mayah, and Will DeMartino for being my home base, and the best friends any one could hope to have.

Susan Whitehead, Paula Steere, Margaret Dinneny for your moral support, friendship, and hair intervention.

Thank you to Pete Wire for taking me hiking when I needed a break from creating, making, writing, and editing (don't pet the cougar), and my "metals posse."

To my family, George, Miles, and Theo: I can depend on you for love, encouragement, and fortitude, and you've never let me down. Thank you with all my heart.

About the Author

CeCe Wire is an artist and metalsmith living in Fort Collins, Colorado. She and her husband enjoy hiking, and take advantage of the Colorado powder for cross-country skiing and snow shoeing. She earned a BFA in 1987 from Kutztown University of Pennsylvania and an MFA in 1995 from Colorado State University. She has more than 10 years of college teaching experience at Colorado State University, the University of Northern Colorado, and Aims Community College, where she earned an Adjunct Faculty Award for Excellence in Teaching in 1997. Workshop teaching has taken her around the globe, including the United Kingdom, Italy, Spain, and Japan. She has been invited repeatedly to teach at the Arrowmont School of Art and Crafts and several prestigious art centers including Peters Valley, The Brookfield Craft Center, and The Mendocino Art Center. Her love of teaching keeps her away from home from the first weekend in February to the first weekend in November. She is actively on the teaching schedules for Made in Metal, Metals Edge, and Metalwerx studios. Her work has been exhibited nationally since 1993, and most recently her metal clay Barns and Silos Series was featured in a group exhibition in Barcelona, Spain. She served as the Executive Director of the Precious Metal Clay Guild, an international organization created to inform, educate, and provide technical assistance for anyone working with metal clay. Her first book, entitled *Creative Metal Clay Jewelry: Techniques, Projects, Inspiration*, was published in 2003, by Lark Books.

Index